Educational Leadership and Declining Enrollments

Lewis B. Mayhew

AND

THE COMMITTEE ON ADMINISTRATION
AND POLICY ANALYSIS

J. Victor Baldridge   William H. Strand
Barbara R. Hatton   Stephen Weiner
Michael W. Kirst   Aaron Gurwitz
Henry M. Levin   Michael J. Korff
James G. March

STANFORD UNIVERSITY

McCutchan Publishing Corporation
2526 Grove Street
Berkeley, California 94704

CONTENTS

iii

FOREWORD

It has been the best of fashion for some time to raise contagious cries of calamity against processes and persons in educational administration. As the negative criticism has grown, the elders in administration have drawn back into a secular priesthood, overly defensive and status-defending. The profession needs Prometheus but it has continued largely to produce Procrustes. Instead of heuristic imagination and reformulation, too frequently it has served up spasms of intemperate empiricism and catchy neologisms. The critics have not done much better—as Gibbon noted, "Corsica" is much easier to deplore than describe.

In this volume, my colleagues present and rationalize a new program for preparing educational administrators. While, admittedly, we are more full-hearted than sure, we attempt a licit marriage of complexity and practicality in the preparation of administrators for a future that isn't what it used to be. We believe that complexity and scholarship have a bright and necessary place in educational administration; we even suspect that they may be fun.

Since the days of Elwood Cubberley and Jesse Sears, the School of Education at Stanford University has produced several generations of educational administrators. All of them have brought credit to their *alma mater*, and a warming number have achieved national and international preeminence. In embarking on the new voyage described here, we are not rejecting our history. On the contrary, our alumni and earlier colleagues have taught us well. Like us (and Thomas Jefferson), they "like the dreams of the future better than the history of the past"; their experience and criticisms have entered significantly in the thinking and proposals presented in the pages that follow. To them go our genuine gratitude and compliments.

Arthur Coladarci

Dean, School of Education
Stanford University

PREFACE

This book is a report of a major curriculum revision undertaken by the faculty in educational administration in the School of Education, Stanford University. Ordinarily such a report would be primarily of parochial interest, and inappropriate for dissemination to a larger audience. However, the Stanford faculty attempted to sense the educational needs of the 1970s and 1980s, to ponder the kinds of administrative services likely to be needed, and to suggest one model that might have applicability beyond Stanford. The curriculum revision was conducted in the context of changes in education for the professions generally, changes detected in professional education and recent policy analyses and pronouncements regarding all American education.

The book is divided into two parts, together with an appendix. Part I contains the rationale for a new program in educational administration, as well as an indication as to how a number of critical issues were resolved. Part II consists of papers and summaries of papers prepared for an Invitational Conference held at Stanford in January 1974. This conference was intended as a means of obtaining reactions from the field of educational administration to what the Stanford faculty was proposing. The appendix presents a set of guidelines and course descriptions for the new program in Educational Administration as envisioned by the faculty after its curriculum study.

    While a single author is shown for this book, it really is a coopera-
tive effort in which the designated author served more as a secretary
recording the ideas of his colleagues, than the sole author of a mono-
graph. It should be acknowledged, however, that while most of the
ideas presented were suggested by colleagues and they have read and
reacted to the manuscript, the interpretation and phrasing of those
ideas is the responsibility of the author, who must assume responsibility for any distortions, inconsistencies, or infelicitous phrasing.

    The assistance of many people is necessary for a cooperative proj-
ect like this one, and an accurate acknowledgment of individual contributions would become burdensomely long. However, specific recognition should be given the Ford Foundation and Ms. Terry Saario
who acted favorably on the unusual proposal to a foundation which
said in essence, The Stanford faculty needs time to talk with each
other—time the members can't seem to free out of their schedules:
"Would you please provide some financing for rather focused conver-
sation?" Acknowledgment is also due Mrs. Phyllis Anderson, who became secretary for the administration faculty just a few weeks before
the curriculum study began. She successfully became acquainted
with the faculty and the many issues it faced, and ensured that the
flow of essential documents was maintained during the planning activity and the actual preparation of this report.

Lewis B. Mayhew

Stanford, California
February 1974

PART I

RATIONALE
FOR CHANGE

An attempt is made in Part I to indicate the nature of professional education generally, the changes that seem to be taking place in professional fields, whether they be law, business, or nursing, and then to indicate the unique problems currently faced by programs designed to train educational administrators. To give point to some of these problems, the peculiar problems faced by the faculty in administration at Stanford are described, and the new Program in Administration which that faculty has developed is set forth. In support of a new program that, in some respects, runs counter to other trends in education for the professions, a rather exhaustive rationale is presented which reveals a consistent faculty point of view toward administration and toward the preparation of administrators. Because the Stanford School of Education is unique among schools of education, a serious attempt is made to indicate which of the elements of the new program are adaptable elsewhere and which are more indigenous to Stanford's problems. Out of this blend of the general and the specific has been contrived a report which we hope will be of value to education faculties throughout the United States.

1. Changing Education for the Professions

Within American society there has developed a unique method for providing required professional services.[1] For a number of professions, formal preparation for future practitioners is conducted in professional schools, lodged administratively and economically in complex university structures. The apprenticeship system of preparing practitioners has largely disappeared in most of the older professions and is rapidly being eradicated as newer vocations seek professional status. Thus professional schools carry a heavy responsibility to the society and to the professions themselves.

The Problems

Properly to assume that responsibility requires the solution of a number of problems, both in the professions and in professional education itself. The first problem is finding objectives for a profession that are acceptable to its members and to the society the profession serves; currently, for example, some would contend that the martial profession has lost its essential validity of purpose. Second is the problem of attaining the uniqueness that is essential for an occupation to qualify as a profession. Uniqueness must come through the educational program that will help those who follow it render a unique service, one which is substantive rather than purely formal. Yet this uniqueness must not degenerate into social withdrawal, a caste status, or special privilege. Thirdly, the profession must win recognition, without which it cannot perform its essential services and without which it cannot select highly qualified potential members. Without recognition, the place of a professional school on a university campus is jeopardized—witness the long struggle of schools of education to be accepted as full partners in the academic world. And without recognition, financial support is hard to acquire and hold.

As professions and professional schools seek recognition, they encounter still another problem—that of standards. Professional service implies service of a special order, requiring competence rigorously tested before the professional is permitted to practice. But this raises such a knotty question as: What connection actually exists between educational standards and professional performance standards? There is increasing evidence of a wide gulf between academic standards as maintained by the professional schools and the actual standards of performance in successful practice.

The matter of standards or quality must be considered conjointly with the problem of supply. Professional schools must seek out and educate enough students to meet demands for service, but the students must be those who can profit from the programs of professional schools. It has been estimated that no more than 10 percent of the population has the ability to be educated for professional service, but this estimate fails both to meet increased societal needs for more professional people and to take into account newer notions about the nature of potential talent. Since professions and professional schools are human institutions, they are inclined to perpetuate older ways of performance even when the times call for radical change. It is hoped that reform can be orderly, but as the Flexner study of medical education showed, sometimes reform is so overdue that genuine trauma must occur to produce it. The Flexner study resulted in the elimination of almost half the medical schools in the country.

A particularly vexing problem for professional education is the balance between theory and skill. Professional service requires mastery of a body of knowledge as well as professional craftsmanship, but the question as to which a professional school should emphasize remains unanswered. There is evidence that a number of professional schools have moved too far in the direction of theory and some reforms now represent attempts to moderate that swing. However, professional schools can and often have erred in the direction of overemphasis on practice, ending up with a "how-to-do-it" procedure which limits members' ability to adapt to changed conditions.

A related problem is that of specialization, including the questions of how much specialization, and at what point preparation for it, should be undertaken. Again, a pendulum-like swing is apparent, with the tendency in one generation for specialization to come early in one's education career, while in the next generation specialization is introduced much later.

Frequently, the professions reveal a conflicting pattern. Thus some engineering educators are arguing for a four-year curriculum of engineering science with specialization either in graduate school or on the job, while at the same time medical education, by making the curriculum more flexible, is encouraging students to begin or at least to anticipate specialization in their first year at medical school. The very fact that professional schools are located in universities raises questions of relationships, and these in turn have curricular significance. The definition of a profession as a self-determining collectivity requires considerable autonomy for the professional school. Yet the university has a stake in, for example, standards of admissions, qualifications of faculty, and characteristics and expense of curriculum. The matter of conferral of degrees is illustrative. According to a purist view of the autonomy of professions, the professional schools should be able to set graduation requirements and determine when students have achieved them. However, the university may wish to impose quality control judgments to ensure that the product of each associated professional school is at least generally the equal of all others. The curricular involvement of this problem is in establishing proper relationships between the professional schools and the college of liberal arts and its graduate school. The university will usually maintain that a reasonably heavy increment of liberal arts education should be part of the experience of each graduate (a frequent proportion is one-third of a total professional program). Such heavy increments reduce time for purely professional work, and are frequently judged inappropriate by professional faculty members when comparable work in the arts and sciences is offered outside the professional school. This has never been an easy problem, but it now seems more insoluble as liberal arts faculties take on many attributes of professional schools and teach their courses with an ultimate professional aim in mind, which may be antithetical to the professional goals of, for example, medicine, law, or home economics. Deeply involved in this matter is the responsibility of educational institutions to prepare citizen-leaders in the attributes of citizenship, presumably derived from the liberal arts and sciences. For its part, the professional school has high interest in producing technically competent practitioners, and at times seems to wish to achieve this at the expense of other educational preparation.

And finally, the professions, and the professional schools, must solve the problems of their relationships with each other and with the subprofessions. There are jurisdictional matters as to who should prepare public administrators—the graduate school of business or the school of engineering? Some professions are frankly competitive for functions, e.g., psychiatry and clinical psychology. As professional services related to complex human problems become more and more interdisciplinary, the problem of relationships will become more acute. Professional practice will increasingly require the services of many workers, paraprofessionals trained somewhat differently than the professional person himself. Engineers, architects, dentists, and teachers all require assistance of various sorts. This raises questions as to who should prepare those assistants and whether some professional assistants should be encouraged to seek full professional recognition. This matter seems particularly pressing in nursing, which now views itself as a profession although its practitioners are typically used at the discretion of and for the service of the medical profession. Also involved is the matter of continuing professional education: who should provide it and how should it be financed? Given the rapid expansion of relevant knowledge for the professions, it seems axiomatic that continuing education is essential. Yet few institutions within the university structure have been able to institutionalize continuing education in all professional fields that require it.

Assuming that these perennial problems are solved, there would still be powerful forces for radical change in professional education. First, it has become apparent that a society as complex as that of the United States must establish national goals at least a decade in advance if it is going to produce the sort of life the people want. Various agencies, government and private, have helped to articulate goals for sixteen national fields:

(1) Agriculture
(2) Area redevelopment
(3) Consumer expenditures
(4) Education
(5) Health
(6) Housing
(7) International aid
(8) Manpower retraining

(9) National defense
(10) Natural resources
(11) Private plant and equipment
(12) Research and development
(13) Social welfare
(14) Space
(15) Transportation
(16) Urban development

Selecting Personnel for the Professions

Lecht finds that "not enough manpower will be available in the decade of the seventies if the American people and their government try to achieve simultaneously all standards that knowledgeable people regard as desirable and reasonable in the various areas identified as national goals." [2]

Even assuming that the manpower was available, the professional schools at present seem unable to create the requisite educational programs for preparing high-level personnel to grapple with these interdisciplinary and interfield problems. Institutions are now struggling to deal with healthy urban development and the proper allocation of natural resources, but as yet no means to solve either has been agreed on. During the 1960s the educational establishment was able to produce the workers needed for achievements in space, but the retraining and redeploying of some of those workers during the 1970s poses a serious administrative and curricular problem.

One of the assumptions on which the edifice of formal professional education is based is that individuals with potential for professional work can be identified, and that the work offered in the professional schools assures successful professional performance. This assumption has recently come into serious question.

Aptitude

Selection for admission into professional schools has been largely based on intelligence or academic aptitude, in the hope that the more intelligent would be the more creative. MacKinnon and others, however, have found little relationship between intelligence and creative achievement. Says MacKinnon:

> As for the relation between intelligence and creativity, save for the mathematicians where there is a low positive correlation between intelligence and the level of creativeness, we have found within our creative samples essentially zero relationship between the two variables, and this is not due to a narrow restriction in the range of intelligence. Among creative architects who have a mean score of 113 on the Terman Concept Mastery Test, individual scores range widely from 39 to 179. Yet scores on this measure of intelligence correlate negatively, —.08, with rated creativity.
>
> Over the whole range of intelligence and creativity there is, of course, a positive relationship between the two variables. No feebleminded subjects have shown up in any of our creative groups. It is clear, however, that above a certain required minimum level of intelligence which varies from field to field, and in some instances may be surprisingly low, being more intelligent does not guarantee a corresponding increase in creativeness. It just is not true that the more intelligent person is necessarily the more creative one.[3]

Historically, successful performance in schools and colleges, including professional ones, has been indicated by grades, on the assumption that success in courses was predictive of successful performance at work. But this also has come into question. After a careful review of most of the available studies of the relationship between college success and postcollege accomplishment, Hoyt generalizes that "we can safely conclude that college grades have no more than a very modest correlation with adult success, no matter how defined. Refinements in experimental methodology are extremely unlikely to alter that generalization. At best they may determine some of the conditions under which a low positive rather than a zero correlation is obtained."[4]

Ivar Berg[5] reinforces this point in an elaborate study of education and job performance in a number of vocations ranging from unskilled, blue-collar to professional and managerial. He finds that by and large the correlation between job performance and length and level of education is minimally positive or slightly negative. If such studies are further validated, professional schools, if they are to continue to warrant the support and regard they have achieved in the past, will be forced into radical revision of the entire process of education, beginning with techniques of admissions and extending to organization of courses and requirements for graduation.

Minority Demands

The third force pressuring professional education to change is the demand by blacks and other culturally deprived minority groups for equal opportunity in American society. For all education, but especially for professional education, this poses several distinct problems. The overall state of cultural and health deprivation in which the large majority of the American black population has been raised has not provided the training and experience needed successfully to survive professional curricula as it is presently offered. Black youth was typically not motivated to seek professional education; hence for many years professional schools did not feel obligated to make specific provision for students with less than adequate backgrounds. Now, however, with a new social ethos which requires professional schools to increase radically the proportion of black youth admitted, the issue appears apposite.

Values

However, even if the difficult matters of admissions, remedial work, financial support, and subsequent entry into the professions were solved, another vexation must be faced. Professional schools evolved in the United States in consonance with the values of Western civilization, and even more narrowly in consonance with white Anglo-Saxon Protestant values. The emerging black community in search of an education—including professional education—that is derivative from their own black cultural experience, has placed demands that are difficult and perhaps impossible to meet in the 1970s. The challenge is eloquently put by the LeMelles, who remark:

> The unprecedented prospect for progressive change in higher education for the black American over the next decade should not obscure the magnitude of the problem. Reorientation of an entire education subsystem cannot be

achieved without painful frustrations and some agony. To obtain genuine and lasting results radically creative steps will have to be taken to give new direction and to compensate both quantitatively and qualitatively for past deficiencies. New leadership and the input of major resources will not suffice to permit the black colleges to attain their true objectives. The tutelary approach to education, which resulted from the worst influences conspiring to miseducate black youth and which has generally characterized a significant segment of traditional Negro educational leadership, is no longer tenable, and more of the same would undoubtedly be disastrous. The fallacy of the mere application of large sums of money to correct complex problems, without fully understanding how such funds should be applied, has been lamentably illustrated in the recently lost war on poverty. The kind of leadership that will perform the innovative role that black higher education needs must be distinctly different from that leadership of the past which accepted the limitations placed upon the status of black Americans. It is for this reason that this book insists that a black educational leadership, distinctly different in its ideals, in its perception of the status of black Americans, and in its willingness to provide new directions, is alone capable of exercising such high responsibility at this critical juncture in the destiny of black America.[6]

Student Unrest

A related force demanding change in professional curricula must be mentioned, although its true significance is as yet unclear. This is the tidal wave of student dissent, protest, and unrest that characterized American college campuses from 1964 to 1970. The student cry for greater relevance in the curriculum would apparently have implications for the professional schools, but this is tempered by the frequently observed fact that protesting students typically came from the nonprofessional schools, especially from the humanities and social sciences, and that the greatest support for existing institutional practices came from such professional fields as medicine, engineering, business, and law.

The Increase in Knowledge

Among the recognized forces driving professional schools to reform is the technological revolution and the exponential increase in
knowledge or relevant information. While the manifestations of these
are legion, the successful attempts of professional fields to respond are
few. As medicine and engineering have discovered, simple expansion of
the time required for professional preparation is no solution. A student
would require a lifetime for even partial coverage of the knowledge being produced today. Nor is more and more refined specialization the
answer. Both the professions and the society need generalists and specialists who can understand the contributions of other specialties.

Thus, professional schools must search for new ways of organizing
information so that students can perceive broad dimensions and develop skills to acquire special knowledge when this is necessary in the
future. They must discover patterns that will provide some general
common preparation, time for specialization, and time to find relationships with other specialties. They must also discover ways of preparing new kinds of generalists, such as doctors' assistants or nurses
turned general practitioners who can provide service or appropriate
referral to patients. And they must find efficient ways of introducing
to the curriculum pertinent knowledge previously unknown or considered esoteric.

Advances like those in the technology and the increase of knowledge, as well as other changes in social structure, call for greater professional services which older ways of training people cannot meet. A
change in political posture regarding human welfare results in a dras-
tic increase in need for social workers beyond the capacity of existing schools. Concentration of the majority of the population in urban areas attracts professional workers but leaves other regions un-
dersupplied yet with increasing expectations for professional services.
The schools must somehow persuade and prepare people to work in
the ghettos, rural areas, and small towns.

How the Problems Affect Schools of Education

Similar problems and forces face schools of education seeking to
prepare educational administrators, and these are expressed in many

different ways. Much of recent educational literature has stressed the training of school teachers but has given relatively little attention to the preparation of administrators. It is increasingly apparent that, regardless of the ability and training of teachers, a poor administrator can frustrate their attempts to do things differently. The administrator has come to play a crucial role in creating the kind of climate in which a teacher is encouraged to be more experimental or to accept new ideas from outside the school. Then, too, the demands of many minority communities for greater school responsiveness to their needs has exposed the inability of administrators to deal with the complexities of community relations. It has also revealed a lack of sensitivity of many administrators to the concerns of minority groups. In addition, the increasing size of the educational enterprise, together with the demand that the schools be held accountable, has focused greater public attention on the school administrators. School principals and superintendents and college presidents must become well versed and skilled in the techniques of management. While at present there is probably an oversupply of credentialed individuals to assume educational administrative positions, there is still great uncertainty about how to select effective administrators or how to prepare them. Despite this, it is essential that institutions preparing administrators must try to bring about some reform with at least a plausible chance of success.

Training Educational Administrators

Educational administrators have traditionally been prepared in colleges of education in which the specific content of required courses changed over time, depending on which among several images of administrators prevailed at the moment. Four general types of administrators have been identified—educational superman, technical manager, democratic leader, and applied social scientist; the most popular view in 1973 was the image of the applied social scientist. There has been considerable dissatisfaction with the training program that is based largely on courses, many of which lack any significant prophetic quality. Because the larger society is changing so radically, educational administrators must be trained not only in technical managerial skills, but also trained to exercise that elusive quality called educational leadership. There has, of course, been some attempt to break away from traditional patterns of training. Some administration programs are based in the whole university rather than in the college of education. In some schools joint degree programs have been adopted, e.g., combining educational administration and law. Some institutions have developed comprehensive internship programs so that the training of administrators will have a major component of reality, and there is apparently great need for in-service education for operating educational administrators that can bring them up-to-date on newer technical or scholarly approaches. Assuming that lay board members of educational institutions are likely to continue to exist, an important element of the administrator's professional life is working with the board of trustees—a board educated to be more sophisticated about educational as well as community problems.

The Decline of the Education Industry

The Carnegie Commission on Higher Education has stressed several problems that will require specific curricular response, and made four specific recommendations:

1. Selection of school administrators is a critical problem on which we need a great deal more research. The profession should be more diverse and should make special efforts to recruit minorities and women.
2. Given a diversity of school districts, there can be no single model of an administrator program. Common elements in all programs should be the use of the resources of the whole university and experimentation with different ways of combining theory and practice in clinical settings.
3. Greater emphasis should be placed on in-service training as a way of keeping administrators up-to-date and as a vehicle for school improvement.
4. Universities in conjunction with state school board associations should experiment with various means of providing school board members with information on crucial issues.[7]

Another view of educational administration reveals a different but nonetheless consistent set of problems.[8] In spite of the fact that educational budgets at all levels continue to increase and expenses to expand, education can be viewed as a declining industry. Certainly the rate of growth since the 1960s has declined and at some levels of education there is an absolute decline in the number of students. The reason for the status of a declining industry is easy to document. The rapid growth in education during the 1950s resulted from the simultaneous increase of the proportion of youth engaged in formal education and the increase in the total number of young people. In the late 1960s, again simultaneously, there came a near saturation of formal education with members of relevant age groups and a sharp drop in the birth rate. A decline in patronage of standard educational programs was the inevitable result.

Declining industries seem to possess common characteristics. When an industry is expanding, managers and administrators are younger because of promotion and mobility possibilities produced through expansion. As growth slows, managers and administrators tend to age and incumbents tend to remain in positions longer. Long tenure in a position, especially in times of dwindling resources, tends to produce lower morale, some cynicism, and considerable doubt as to the essential worthwhileness of the enterprise. Still, incumbents guard their positions tenaciously for they are faced with an oversupply of qualified or at least credentialed administrators. As is true of so many segments of the trained labor market, the process by which administrators are produced is not controlled soon enough, or fast enough, or hard enough to avoid serious overproduction. Such overproduction can have any of several consequences. The availability of large numbers of younger, and possibly better qualified, administrators can produce anxiety, conservatism, and unwillingness to take chances in incumbents. However, because one view of educational systems is that they exist in large measure to provide work opportunities for relevantly trained individuals, a second consequence of overproduction could be the creation of administrative superstructures, such as statewide coordinating systems or other governmental and organizational bureaucracies which can provide career opportunities. An examination of the career paths of graduates of the growing number of collegiate programs in the administration of higher education seems to illustrate this phenomenon. Many recent graduates are absorbed in recently created state coordinating councils, regional contracts, consortia, national professional associations, and newly formed staffs for federal programs.

Loss of Public Confidence

A particular perplexity is that, along with the numerical decline of clients for the education industry, there has come a loss of public confidence in education. During the 1950s and much of the 1960s high public expectations were generated as to what formal education could do. James Perkins called the university the pivotal institution in American society, and President Johnson's White House Conference on Education saw education as the principal instrument for the achievement of national policy. It was assumed that education could eliminate the technological lead that Russia demonstrated through the launching of Sputnik. Education, both higher and lower, was expected to eliminate racial and sexual inequities, the problems of the cities, and improve markedly the quality of American life. Expecting great things, the public poured belief and financial support into the educational enterprise. But then came disillusion. The educational system was not successful in meeting those expectations. It had little impact on racial or sexual inequalities. It did not affect the quality of life in cities or the tone of social morality. Actually, of course, such failures should have been expected, and educational leaders in particular should not have contributed to raising public expectations of what schools and colleges can do. A society that wishes to eliminate unemployment or slums addresses those problems directly, not indirectly through education. What seems likely is that social expectations as well as support for education will continue to decline, and the environment in which schools and colleges function may become either indifferent or hostile or both. Yet schools and colleges are an essential ingredient in a developed society, if for no other reason than to serve as a relatively inexpensive and not too destructive system for the custodial care of those whom the labor market is not yet ready to receive. Educational managers and administrators must in some way be prepared to function in such a "bear market" environment.

This matter may be viewed a different way. It is quite possible that education may be entering the third of a series of phases in the history of any social institution. The first stage is one of dynamic growth; social expectations rise, there is excitement, expansion, and self-confidence and the institution is able to meet or seem to meet those expectations. The second stage is one of conflict as social ex-

pectations exceed the capabilities of the institution; there is frustration, anger, and recrimination exemplified by, for example, sharp increases in proposed vindictive legislation. The third period is one of
neglect, reduced expectations, indifference, passivity, and stagnation.
The expansionist phase is a happy one for managers and administrators and for those agencies and institutions that prepare them for
their roles. Training programs produce credentialed administrators
who succeed each year in increasing budgets, expanding physical
plants, and enriching programs. The temptation to reach the conclusion that the training program directly influenced those good things
is almost irresistible. That euphoria quickly ends during the period
of conflict as problems proliferate and persist indefinitely. Managers,
administrators, and those who prepare them conduct frenzied
searches for solutions to problems but the grail they once felt they
had found eludes them. The third period, that of neglect, may ease
the frenzy of the quest but produces other concerns which properly
should be addressed. Administrators face a reduced social role and
esteem, and must be prepared to do so. Numerical and financial
growth has stopped yet educational institutions must be kept somewhat innovative and responsive to changing conditions in other portions of the society. Managers and administrators must be prepared
to make more effective use of dwindling resources even if it is true
that education is moving into a period of neglect. A defeatist attitude
would be highly inappropriate. Administration can be viewed as the
profession of leadership and the art of intelligently coping with an
arbitrary fate. In many respects the prospects for human control over
events are dependent on collections of minor matters, and educational administrators and managers should be prepared to exist professionally without eminence and to deal effectively with those
minor matters that in aggregate often make a difference.

"Organized Anarchy"

One concept that might clarify the dilemma of educational administrators and at the same time suggest how they can function with
reasonable effectiveness is that of "organized anarchy." An anarchic
organization is a social institution whose goals are problematic, obscure, and conflicting. What technologies may be available to reach
that unknown state is also unclear and little understood. Further,

few techniques are available to evaluate the achievement of these unclear goals sought through imprecise technologies. The concept of
organized anarchy is not necessarily negative, nor does it imply that
large-scale examples, such as education, are expendable. Schools and
colleges are an essential part of American life; if they are anarchic
organizations, then those who prepare people to function in them
should be responsible for developing skills necessary at least to cope
with and possibly to control their institutions. Eight skills can be
identified that might provide one dimension of an outline for a training program for educational administrators:

(1) Peer skills: the ability to establish and maintain a network of con-
    tacts with equals;
(2) Leadership skills: the ability to deal with subordinates and the
    complications of authority, power, and dependence;
(3) Conflict resolution skills: the ability to mediate conflict, handle
    disturbances, and work under psychological stress;
(4) Information-processing skills: the ability to build networks, ex-
    tract and validate information, and disseminate information ef-
    fectively;
(5) Skills in unstructured decision-making: the ability to find prob-
    lems and solutions when alternatives, information and objectives
    are ambiguous;
(6) Resource-allocation skills: the ability to decide among alternative
    uses of time and other organizational resources;
(7) Entrepreneurial skills: the ability to take sensible risks and imple-
    ment innovations;
(8) Skills of introspection: the ability to understand the position of
    manager and its impact on the organization.

Observing the Existing Trends

On the assumption that educational institutions are reactive, one
can at least infer problems and perplexities through observing experiments, trends, and developments in institutions that prepare educational administrators. In, for example, content of courses and curricula, there is a definite attempt to include theoretical, conceptual,
and research-based materials drawn from the social and behavioral
sciences. Presumably rooted in such a base but possibly incongruent
with that development is the effort to enrich programs by teaching
such skills as the use of data processing, coping with teacher mili-

tancy and collective negotiations, dealing with the indigenous problems of urban education, and utilizing emergent management technologies. It should be pointed out that relatively few courses oriented toward those problems are listed in school of education cata-
logs nor is there a significant cadre of experts who can teach these
new specialized skills. But the interest in them indicates a cluster of
new concerns that in some way or other must be accommodated in
curricula for the future.

Program structure seems to require modification through providing greater flexibility while at the same time increasing internal structure in preparatory programs. The flexibility, of course, is intended
to allow students to tailor their studies to their own career objectives, whereas greater structure is intended to facilitate integration
through ensuring sequence and balance among program elements. A
somewhat different structural matter is the need for better working
relationships between departments of educational administration and
university divisions outside the school. For too long schools of education have operated in an isolated and subordinate role vis-à-vis
other schools and colleges. In part this situation was brought about
because professors in other parts of the university would not interest
themselves in educational concerns. Gradually, however, it has become apparent that if school administrators—or for that matter
teachers—are to receive the rich kind of professional preparation they
require, other parts of the university should be called upon to make
significant contributions.

Expanding Recruitment of Talented Candidates

Although all professional schools are responsible for recruiting
enough capable individuals to ensure an adequate supply of newly
trained practitioners, there seems to be an especial need for schools
of education to make more systematic and aggressive efforts to recruit talented persons into their programs. To achieve this will require expanding the traditional recruitment pool for candidates for
advanced preparation in educational administration. Part of the expanded pool will be younger, less experienced educators—persons
with training and/or experience in areas other than education, members of disadvantaged minority groups, and those who live beyond
the geographic boundaries of the university's service area. As the
pool of candidates is expanded there will be need for greater involve-

ment of practicing administrators to nominate candidates, need for increased financial assistance to students—especially disadvantaged minority groups and women, need for more rigorous intellectual screening standards, and for more valid selection procedures to predict ultimate successful administrative performance. Quite possibly the insights of practicing administrators could be used more frequently in selecting candidates for doctoral programs.

Shifts in Educational Methods

The instructional approaches now being attempted in programs for educational administrators are remarkably similar to approaches being undertaken in other professional schools, and for substantially the same reasons. There is a clear tendency away from traditional lecture-textbook methods and toward using a variety of audiovisual media, reality-oriented materials, and alternative instructional strategies. Most prevalent is the use of simulation case studies, seminars, and team teaching. There is a powerful push toward creating more and better field-related experiences such as internships and participation in surveys by students. These instructional innovations stand as eloquent testimony to the previous lack of reality orientation of so many administrator training programs.

Related in a sense, but also different, is the trend toward increased sophistication in student research, including more consistent theoretical bases, more elegant designs, and the use of advanced methodologies and statistical analyses. Along with this are the trends toward more programmatic research by teams of students and professors and toward providing students with many more pre- or non-dissertation research opportunities. All of this is intended to increase flexibility so that students can select research topics that are consistent with their own interests and talents. An important subcategory is that of facing students with realistic problems like those administrators deal with and asking them to approach those problems from a research point of view.

Requirements for graduation are changing, albeit slowly, in response to new circumstances or to final perception of abuse or ineffectiveness of a practice. Thus, a period of full-time residence increasingly is being required to overcome the abuse of administrator training that has come about through part-time and summer accumulation of credits. Foreign language examinations are rapidly being eliminated on the ground that they are essentially irrelevant to the needs of American educational administrators. In place of the foreign language requirement, work outside the school of education is often required, in such disciplines as statistics and research design. Serious efforts are also being made to increase the flexibility of requirements for graduation so that within a single broad program a number of subspecialties can be accommodated, allowing students to select individualized patterns of courses and experiences. In a few institutions, feelings about fieldwork are so strong that a formal internship or field-related experience has been made a requirement.

Although the movement is still tenuous, there is a great deal of discussion of the need for more thorough, continuous, and systematic evaluation of preparatory programs for educational administrators. Attempts are being made to observe recent graduates in the field to obtain feedback information and in general to provide a more solid base for judging programs than sheer quantitative output provides. Should the much-publicized demand in the early 1970s for greater educational accountability be realized, formal evaluation of programs is likely to become a major preoccupation of all levels and types of education, including education for educational administrators.

Trends in staffing departments of educational administration are in flux and frequently contradictory. There is some interest in adding professors with definite specialties, rather than continuing the practice of appointing generalists with considerable administrative experience in schools. In most institutions there is a conscious effort to increase the number of professors coming from the several relevant academic disciplines in order to improve the balance between research-oriented and practice-oriented professors. However, in a few there has been a counter swing when it was discovered that departments are so overloaded with discipline-oriented professors that viable contacts with the field are no longer possible. A small but potentially significant trend is for schools of education to provide for or to create special preservice or continuing education programs for professors of educational administration, on the assumption that the half-life of many subjects germane to the preparation of educational administrators and managers is substantially less than the average tenure of professors. This retreading seems especially to be warranted.

Particularly if the slowdown in the education industry is real, then substantial increases in the amount and quality of in-service programs for practicing administrators become necessary. Summer workshops, short courses, conferences, will all be designed to bring administrators up-to-date on such emergent problems as collective bargaining or simulated planning. This in-service training will require more than just the resources of the university, for it will require the cooperation of practicing administrators and other agencies such as professional associations, local school districts, state education departments, and federally funded centers. The form of continuing education will be varied, with some long-term residential programs for superintendents, e.g., retreats or postdoctoral opportunities on campus. There is also a need to take education to where administrators are, through, for example, consulting services, field services, and credit courses offered by the university but located in specific school systems. Increasingly, efforts are being made to correlate these various continuing education activities into an integrated and interactive whole.

Further Specialization in the Profession

One last background factor of considerable significance for the preparation of educational administrators must be mentioned. In previous decades, schools of education held narrow concepts of the kinds of roles their graduates would occupy. The standard administrative roles of principal, superintendent, and state superintendent of public instruction were only slightly augmented by such roles as curriculum coordinator or district budget officer. During the 1950s and 1960s, however, the number of agencies and institutions directly involved with education increased, thereby placing demands for new kinds of specialists on schools of education. First, the number and variety of staff offices in districts and educational systems increased to include such new subspecialties as institutional research, offices of planning, and offices of management information systems. Various state and federal agencies expanded their responsibility for educational matters and required new kinds of staff members such as policy analysts. Proprietary and special purpose institutions have grown in number and these require still different sorts of administrative skills and talents. The increasingly significant function of planning, budget, and space allocation, community relations, legal relations, as well as political relations require new sorts of individuals who, presumably, could be trained if schools of education were able to modify their programs suitably. There is nothing inconsistent in this expansion of the scope of educational activities, which should be the concern of schools of education, with the observation made earlier that a definite slowdown in the education industry is possible. For example, even if collegiate enrollments stabilized, as seems likely, by 1980 at the level of eleven or twelve million students, this still presents a much larger and more complex undertaking than was true, for example, in 1952 when all college enrollments totaled two-and-a-half million students. The sheer administrative overhead to coordinate such a large enterprise in a noncentralized fashion prescribes the need for more and more different specialists, to be prepared largely through existing programs.

Notes

1. Background material on problems and issues in professional education is adapted from Lewis B. Mayhew and Patrick J. Ford, *Reform in Graduate and Professional Education* (San Francisco: Jossey-Bass, 1973).

2. Leonard A. Lecht, *Manpower Needs for National Commerce in the 1970s* (New York: Praeger Publishers, 1969).

3. Donald W. MacKinnon, *"The Nature and Nurture of Creative Talent,"* in *Discovery of Talent,* ed. by Dael Wolfle (Cambridge, Mass.: Harvard University Press, 1969), pp. 192-193.

4. Donald P. Hoyt, *The Relationship Between College Graduates and Adult Education: A Review of the Literature* (Iowa City, Ia.: American College Testing Program, 1965), p. 45.

5. Ivar Berg, *Education and Jobs: The Great Training Robbery* (New York: Praeger Publishers, 1970).

6. Tilden J. LeMelle and Wilburt LeMelle, *The Black Colleges: A Strategy for Relevancy* (New York: Praeger Publishers, 1969), pp. 15, 16.

7. Carnegie Commission on Higher Education, *Continuity and Discontinuity: Higher Education and the Schools* (New York: McGraw-Hill, 1973), p. 632.

8. The discussion on pages 13-17 has been adapted from James G. March, "Analytical Skills and the University Training of Educational Administrators," prepared as the Seventh Annual Walter Cocking Memorial Lecture, Bellingham, Wash., 1973.

2. Context for Change at Stanford

The Background

The educational administrator training program in the School of Education at Stanford faces all the issues and perplexities that confront education for the professions, and more specifically education for administrators. In addition, the program must accommodate elements in its own history and the judgment of its own students and alumni. The Stanford School of Education has long been active in the preparation of educational leaders, as is evidenced by the primacy in the study of educational administration of such individuals as Elwood Cubberley, the first director and then dean of the Stanford School of Education. During most of its history, the administrator program was intensely oriented toward field practice and contributed much to the administrative leadership of schools, school systems, and state departments of education in the West. By the early 1960s, the program, although quite decentralized and idiosyncratic, did possess a substantial cadre of professors actively preparing administrative leaders and actively carrying on field services, consultative services, and elaborate summer programs in continuing education. In 1962 there were eleven faculty members devoting major proportions of time to the preparation of administrators, all save one with substantial experience as a practicing administrator. One had been superintendent and another deputy superintendent of large city school systems. Four had been superintendents of medium-sized school districts, and one of that group had also been the chief financial officer for a state public school system. One had been a college president, another the chief academic officer of a university, and two others had had considerable experience in student personnel staff offices. These former practitioners maintained extensive individual counseling activities and also directed a number of programs on campus of direct significance to practicing administrators. In the academic year 1962-1963, for example, the second phase of a six-year internship program for preparing secondary school administrators ended. At about the same time a junior college leadership training program, designed to prepare administrators for community colleges, and a community college planning center, to help plan the anticipated expansion in facilities, were just beginning. The School Planning Laboratory had become the West Coast branch of the Educational Facilities Laboratory, and over the succeeding several years expended budgets in excess of $5 million to help administrators plan their schools and campuses more effectively. There was a reasonably comprehensive administrative field services unit, completely self-sustaining, which provided consultative services throughout the western region. Several large-scale research projects were carried out, such as the examination of the financing of educational systems in the nation's largest cities and surveys of the state of Massachusetts and for the city of Philadelphia.

By 1972, a substantial change had occurred. Most of the administratively experienced professors had died, retired, or moved elsewhere. Only three of the corps from 1962 remained, one of whom was scheduled for retirement in 1973 and the other in 1974. Of the replacements, none had prior experience in the school of education, only one had formal academic preparation in education, none had experience as a chief administrative officer, and one had experience as a third-echelon administrative officer in a university. By this time the various field-related projects had disappeared and the summer session, which in 1962 had enrolled large numbers of practicing administrators, had deteriorated to only a few courses offered to small numbers of students. The new faculty was highly committed and involved in research, much of which had applied implications. In spite of this apparent bias away from the actual practice of administration, the Stanford faculty was quite conscious of its obligations and began seriously to redress the staffing imbalance. At the same time, the faculty began to ponder how it could use its own resources—with hopes that they would be augmented by more representation from the field—to offer a program that would produce administrative officers and leaders. That desire led to the major curriculum restudy which is the substance of this report.

Malfunctions in the Program

Even before the faculty in educational administration began a systematic review of its program, a number of malfunctionings had become apparent. There was no particular rationale for the particular collection of courses and experiences offered, other than the idiosyncratic interests of faculty members and the fact that certain labels for courses were required for state credentialing. Students were able to complete the required number of hours for a degree without necessarily developing a sense of cohesiveness about the field of educational administration as a whole. Such rather casual course offerings did not provide enough in-depth work for people in different specializations. In the past, there had been specializations in higher education, general school administration, school planning, and school finance. In the absence of any common core of work which would be basic to all those specializations, professors interested in each area felt constrained to offer certain basic work and a small amount of advanced work. On reflection, it was assumed that better utilization of faculty resources could result in more intensive work in whatever specializations the faculty authorized. Then, too, students manifested a great deal of uneasiness about the lack of specific skills which they believed administrators should possess and without which they felt they would have difficulty finding employment, especially in an increasingly tight labor market. To a certain extent, this uneasiness could be attributed to general anxiety about the job market, but some of it came to be seen as a valid criticism that the program as so organized—or perhaps disorganized—mitigated against the development of reasonably salable skills. It also became apparent that the program at Stanford did not lead logically to the development of a dissertation proposal and the completion of a thesis congruent with actual course work. Students typically took courses in order of convenience and after course work was finished shifted direction to search out a plausible and easily completed dissertation topic. It was assumed that greater structure and logic for the entire curriculum could conceivably rectify that fault. With such an idiosyncratic collection of courses, the program in administration in the School of Education at Stanford obviously did not generate and produce the common universe of discourse between students and students, and students and faculty, in the sense that the first year of law school produced a common universe of discourse in that corner of the campus. People studying for careers in higher education felt themselves to be isolated from those working in general school administration. Because the course offerings were idiosyncratic to individual professors and had been inserted into the catalog with only perfunctory approval and no examination of interrelationships between courses, the curriculum came to show considerable redundance. Further, the courses and combinations of them were not designed to make logical use of other parts of the school of education, for example, history, philosophy, guidance, or psychological study.

Student Opinion

These general faculty impressions of the program were substantially validated by a questionnaire study of fifty-two students enrolled in some variant of the administration program at Stanford in spring 1973. That study revealed a reasonably clear profile of the student body and a catalog of opinions on the strengths and weaknesses of the program, and students' desires with respect to it. There were fifty male and two female students; and forty-two nonminority and ten minority students. Slightly more than half were specializing in general school administration, almost a third in higher education, and the remainder were involved in such things as a joint program conducted with the graduate school of business. Two-thirds of the students had received a master's degree before enrolling in Stanford and the group had a mean of almost seven years' experience before entering their graduate program. Eighty-four percent had matriculated for a Ph.D. program, representing a rather substantial shift from the early 1960s, when an equal number were headed toward the Ed.D. degree. The student body was almost evenly divided between those who had and those who had not applied to other graduate schools of education and were seemingly most attracted by the general reputation of the university or the School of Education and the fact that the program in administration appeared to be compatible with their needs. If their plans materialize they expect to spend between three-and-a-half and four years from the time they began course work to the time they receive their advanced degree. After receiving their degrees, the majority (61.5 percent) plan to enter educational administration, which is also their ultimate career objective.

Students' Expectations

The opinions of these students reveal a partially faithful portrait of the program as compared to the perceptions of the faculty and also indicate matters worthy of specific consideration. After arriving at Stanford, these students discovered that the quality of teaching, the competition from other students, and the rigor of course work was approximately what they had expected. However, faculty advising, financial aid, and the integration and consistency of the curriculum fell below expectations. It seems likely that students' expectations of financial aid in graduate school had been conditioned by the expansionist period of the 1960s during which the mythology held that every student could and would receive rather lush scholarships, fellowships, or assistantships. The fact that they experienced less integration and consistency of curriculum is beyond doubt a product of the idiosyncratic program already mentioned. With respect to quality of teaching, effectiveness of faculty advising, student-faculty interaction outside the classroom, and student-student interaction outside the classroom, these students viewed the school of education as like other institutions they had attended or other schools at Stanford. (The one modest deviation from this generalization was the slight tendency to view faculty-student interaction as worse than encountered elsewhere.) This same uniformity appeared in the degree of student satisfaction or dissatisfaction with various elements of the program. There was considerable satisfaction with the intellectual skills of the faculty and considerable dissatisfaction with the orientation of new students into the program. There was minimal satisfaction with the preparation they were receiving for their career objectives and with the opportunities for social interaction with other students. The students were somewhat more satisfied with the intellectual skills of their peers, the teaching of the faculty, and the fact that there was student representation on the committee responsible for the program in administration.

Differences with the Faculty

There appears to be some slight lack of congruence on what elements of the program students judged to be very important and what the faculty considered to be of prime significance. The students assigned the ranking of very important to school finance, organizational theory, school budgeting and accounting, school law, and the politics of education. Gauged of less importance were training in research techniques, economics, curriculum development, and statistics. On a scale of from one (not important) to seven (very important), the median judgments for several other elements were as follows: tests and measurements, 3.9; personnel problems, 5.4; quantitative decision-making techniques, 4.7; management information systems, 5.1; interpersonal dynamics, 5.0; and value conflicts, 4.8. When asked how well they believed various courses or course fields were preparing them for their anticipated roles as competent administrators, these students judged as adequate or more than adequate organizational theory, politics of education, curriculum development, statistics, value conflicts, management information systems, interpersonal dynamics, economics, and tests and measurements. Tending to be judged inadequate were school budgeting and accounting (probably because those matters are not taught in the Stanford program in the traditional sense), school law (probably because it has not been offered in recent years by a trained individual), and personnel problems, including collective bargaining (probably because several matters simply have not been given explicit attention).

These judgments are reflected in Table 2-1. Students find many subjects to be of importance for their preparation as administrators, with statistics and tests and measurements gauged as somewhat less than significant. They are less enthusiastic about the adequacy of how these various subjects are developed at Stanford and are evidently quite dissatisfied with the adequacy of work in budgeting and accounting, school law, and dealing with personnel problems.

Table 2-1. Perceived Importance and Perceived Adequacy
        of Preparation at Stanford

	Median						
	1	2	3	4	5	6	7

1. School finance
        Importance 5.5
        Adequacy   3.8
2. Organizational theory
        Importance 5.6
        Adequacy   4.2
3. Research techniques
        Importance 4.3
        Adequacy   3.8
4. Budgeting and accounting
        Importance 5.5
        Adequacy   2.4
5. Economics
        Importance 4.4
        Adequacy   3.7
6. School law
        Importance 5.6
        Adequacy   2.7
7. Politics of education
        Importance 5.6
        Adequacy   4.6
8. Curriculum development
        Importance 5.0
        Adequacy   3.8
9. Statistics
        Importance 4.2
        Adequacy   4.0
10. Tests and measurements
        Importance 3.9
        Adequacy   3.6
11. Personnel problems
        Importance 5.4
        Adequacy   2.7

Median

1	2	3	4	5	6	7

12. Quantitative decision-making
    Importance 4.7
    Adequacy   3.2
13. Management information systems
    Importance 5.1
    Adequacy   3.6
14. Interpersonal dynamics
    Importance 5.0
    Adequacy   3.5
15. Value conflicts
    Importance 4.8
    Adequacy   4.4

Comments

Student write-in comments point to relatively few elements of the program which they believe should be considerably changed. Their comments are not dissimilar to those which graduate students have long been making. Qualifying examinations should either be abolished or else be more closely related to student interests. Orals should be so designed as to be effective as a screening or diagnostic tool and not the traumatic ritual they currently are. Greater flexibility in topic and type of approach for dissertations should be fostered and dissertations of more direct concern to the practitioner should be encouraged.

The comments of one recent graduate and one student fairly well into his dissertation work seem to reflect general student opinion. The graduate says: "I have noted that many doctoral candidates at Stanford who desire to pursue administrative careers in primary and secondary education express frustration and even anger about the nature of the current training program. These students by and large believe that the faculty is concerned with research and national and state policy analysis, and has little interest in school district level administration and the students who wish to pursue careers at the district level." (While it would be unwise to ignore that frustration, it would be equally unwise to assign too much attention to the day-to-day problems facing local schools.) "I would argue that a certain degree of tension and divergence of view between Stanford and current school administrators is essential to a training program that aspires to produce future administrators who will work for change. Stanford needs to avoid the extremes of being totally out of contact with school districts on the one hand and being submissive allies of such districts on the other." Referring to another matter which perplexes all professional schools, this student remarked that "there must be a much greater effort to bring faculty members into a dialog with students on the moral and ethical problems that arise in administration." One possible means to achieve that would be to ensure that "there be a stronger sense of community among faculty and students . . . . As a student in the business school, I was impressed by the intensity of contact and communication among students. That intensity, I think, represents a very important element in the educational experience."

Six Goals

Understandably, a student still in the program is more concerned with details although he does not overlook the broader needs indicated by the graduate. This individual suggested six goals:

(1) Students should be prepared for future stages of the program. The sequence of courses should be contemplated. Courses should prepare students for internships and dissertations.
(2) Graduates should be prepared for a job, "by ensuring they have requisite knowledge and skills and by facilitating their marketability through improved placement activities."
(3) Graduates should be knowledgeable about education. This knowledge includes the nature, scope, and history of education, plus the pertinent insights and frameworks provided by traditional academic disciplines.
(4) The program itself should be a meaningful experience. Students should have significant contact with professors, peers, and educational leaders and should come to enjoy learning.
(5) The prestige of the program should be enhanced. The prestige of this particular program within Stanford throughout the Bay Area and among programs in higher education and educational administration at other universities is important.
(6) Graduates should have a commitment to the improvement of education.

A student discussion in May 1973 indicated this student's yearning for a kind of educational evangelism and for a more perceivable ethos for the school of education.

Alumni Opinions

Alumni represent one of the most important constituencies with which collegiate institutions must relate. Alumni in their professional roles personify the institution. They also serve as critics and cate-chists for the alma mater, pointing out needed changes. Additionally, they are, or can be, an important source for financing and an extremely important resource for aid in recruitment. As the faculty in administration at Stanford began revision of the program, it turned quite naturally to alumni of the program to determine who they were professionally and what they believed would be helpful components of a program for the future. One hundred forty-one respondents to a questionnaire mailed in the early summer of 1973 provided the information on which generalizations are based. The majority of these former students graduated between 1955 and 1970: 72 percent of them received the Ed.D. degree and 25 percent the Ph.D. Three-quarters of this group obtained their degrees in the field of general school administration, which is a somewhat different balance than for more recent graduates. Degree recipients between 1968 and 1973 were distributed 29 percent in general school administration and 43 percent in higher educational administration. Graduates of the program were, on an average, forty years old when they received their degrees, which generally took them five or more years to earn. A third are presently employed in public schools, almost 42 percent in colleges and universities, 10 percent in the private sector, 7 percent in state or federal government, and 8 percent in miscellaneous activities such as county offices, foundations, or educational special interests groups. Stanford graduates appear to be well remunerated; slightly over one-fourth have incomes of $30,000 or more and almost a half indicated incomes of between $20,000 and $30,000.

To obtain alumni opinion as to the value of various parts of the program at Stanford, respondents were asked to judge value of each along a scale from one (not necessarily critical to success) to seven (absolutely critical to success). Although graduates employed in different settings, e.g., public schools as opposed to colleges and universities, revealed some slight differences of opinion, there was substantial agreement. Those elements of the program judged to be of great value for successful professional practice, as indicated by a mean scale score of five or higher, were school finance, school law, politics of education, personnel problems, written communications, oral communications, interpersonnel dynamics, and community relations. At the other end of the continuum were statistics, tests and measurements, child and adolescent development, anthropology, and micro and macroeconomics. The response pattern is understandable, for most of the respondents are in active administrative positions and they received their graduate education at a time when the administrative faculty was heavily field oriented. They were enrolled when all students at Stanford were required to take a not-too-popular core of three courses in psychology (heavily statistical and experimental), two courses in social foundations (one of which was anthropological), and two out of three electives including history, philosophy, and health. Students in administration were very critical of that core as irrelevant to their real professional concerns, contrasting sharply with the highly relevant courses in school finance, school law, and faculty personnel policies. What is more difficult to gauge is the degree to which their opinions should influence decisions on the curriculum for the future. Statistics, tests and measurements, and macro and microeconomics pose an especial quandary. Quantification-based decision-making seems increasingly to be an essential tool of administration. It appears that if the two movements of increased demand—for accountability and for better methods of assessment, especially for minority group members—persist, then sophisticated understanding of tests and measurements should probably be part of the intellectual equipment of educational administrators.

The Curriculum: Prescribed or Elective?

The faculty for administration at Stanford had to face and resolve a number of curricular issues, most of them endemic in schools of education and other professional schools across the nation, but each conditioned by indigenous conditions and history at Stanford. Perhaps the most universal curricular issue, and the one with the longest history in American education generally, is whether the curriculum should be prescribed or elective. In recent times, the Stanford School

of Education has fluctuated wildly, from an almost chaotic free elective system in the early 1950s, to a substantial core of prescribed
courses in the early 1960s, to the somewhat modified set of requirements adopted during the late 1960s. During the elective period,
each professor was allowed to work out with each student an individual pattern of courses. This freedom produced substantial variation
in the rigor and comprehensiveness of individual programs. Some faculty members were overly generous in allowing a program to be largely comprised of independent study and field experience, which in
practice too often turned out to be assigning academic credit for considerable paid work experience. To correct such abuses, the School
of Education faculty adopted a core that consisted of three terms of
psychological studies, two terms of social foundations of education,
and two courses from among three specified—history, philosophy, or
health. These courses, required of all students, were the basis for
searching qualifying examinations. On the assumption that those
courses provided a measure of quality control, faculty members and
students were allowed to decide independently the composition of
the remainder of each student's program. However, criticisms
mounted. Many students believed that the courses in psychological
studies as taught stressed the research interests of the faculty and
were not concerned with real-life problems as anticipated by aspiring
practitioners. Further, students complained that qualifying examinations were needlessly preoccupied with trivia taken from footnotes in
textbooks and did not allow students to relate what they were learning to genuine educational problems. As a compromise, the faculty
created a new set of requirements intended to ensure only that students had an opportunity to develop some broad competencies.
These requirements were that students should have some course
work in the practices of education, in the social and behavioral sciences, in skills of inquiry, in normative studies, and in both a major
and a minor field of concentration. Students could satisfy those requirements by electing from a range of courses presumably having
relevance for each area. While individual professors were allowed to
work out with each student the remainder of the program, the
School of Education divided its faculty into area committees, which,
in principle, could modify professorial prerogative through stating
area requirements. The administration faculty, renamed the Committee on Administration and Organization Studies, moved gradually

from laissez-faire for each professor to a set of requirements comprised of segments of courses being offered by three faculty members. All students were required to take one course in organizational theory, two courses in economics and finance, and one or two courses in the politics of education. However, these courses were taught discretely and there was little effort to integrate them. Further, some students in specialized concentrations felt that such a core did not give adequate attention to their own unique professional concerns.

Three Options

As the faculty undertook a serious reconsideration of its curriculum, it was faced with at least three viable options with respect to the prescribed-elective dilemma. First, it could continue the program essentially as it was with the modest requirements in organization theory, economics, and politics. That option had the advantage of flexibility, apparently one of the reasons students have been attracted to Stanford, and the added virtue of using already existing courses would place no additional drain on the small faculty overloaded with advising students on dissertation and career problems. This solution, however, contained weaknesses in addition to the one of alleged irrelevance. A required core taught by only three members of an eight-member faculty underutilized some faculty members and overutilized others; obviously, such a core did not expose all students to the full range of interests and talents reflected in the faculty.

A second option was the removal of all requirements, excepting those broad, general ones imposed by the School of Education itself. Such a free elective system could make the program even more flexible than it had been and was highly consistent with the developments in other professional schools that had created virtually a free elective system. The Medical School at Stanford, in theory at least, requires no courses; rather, programs are developed according to the career interests of each student and the judgment of his adviser. However, a free elective system provides no assurance that any two students will develop comparable points of view about administration, nor that graduates will possess even a rudimentary common universe of discourse. The free elective system tends further to fragment the faculty and student body as each "does his own thing," an extravagance ill affordable, especially in a time of financial stringency.

The third option was to develop a somewhat larger and more pre-scribed core of courses that would be taken by all students who matriculated in the programs offered by the Committee on Adminis-tration and Organization Studies. Once a core of courses and experi-ences were agreed on and developed, several quite distinctive concen-trations could be based on that core.

This third alternative could be defended in several different ways. While different administrative specialties and subspecialties require discrete skills and attributes, all administrative roles still seem to re-quire some skills and competencies in common which could be per-haps most effectively developed through a core of exercises, courses, and experiences. It is assumed that, regardless of specific future pro-fessional roles, all students should develop such specific competen-cies as: (1) the ability to speak and write about administrative prob-lems and to do so with reasonable sophistication; (2) the ability to read, understand, and apply research findings relevant to administra-tive and organizational problems and issues; (3) the ability to concep-tualize a reasonably complex research project; (4) the ability to make critical evaluations and judgments about administrative problems and issues; (5) possession of a broad awareness and understanding of rele-vant, descriptive, critical research, and evaluative literature; (6) the ability to define and solve problems dealing with such professional concerns as curricula, finance, organization, teaching, personnel af-fairs, etc.; (7) the ability to discriminate between central problems and issues and those of less significance or peripheral concern; (8) the ability to conceptualize and to reason from a variety of relevant problems; (9) the possession of an understanding of the technical re-quirements for all administrative positions; and (10) the ability to perceive and act on value implications of administrative practices and processes.

The Required Core Curriculum

Several rationales were available to support the required core cur-riculum. One posits a curriculum consisting of three component parts. The first component is a collection of common learning or studies presumed to be needed by all individuals in a major category of education. These learnings provide a common universe of dis-course, a common body of allusion, illustration, and principle and common modes of thought. In undergraduate education, general education requirements have been the devices used for this purpose. In a graduate program in administration, the common learnings would be those materials apparently needed by all involved in the administration and organization of education. Secondly, there should be a collection of studies and experiences designed primarily to broaden an individual's intellectual horizons. Some of these studies could be taken out of sheer curiosity, or to extend the implications of more concentrated learning. Thirdly, there should be a collection of courses and experiences that properly could be called contextual studies. These studies provide the context within which a specific concentration could be developed. Contextual studies could be offered in the undergraduate program through, for example, economics and political science, to provide the context for a major in history, or physics, chemistry, and mathematics, providing the context for engineering. For a program in educational administration, the context might be sociology, political science, and economics.

Another rationale for a core curriculum can be arrived at by considering academic degree structures. In general, it seems wise to limit the number of specific academic degrees, but each degree should be flexible enough to allow several different tracks through the requisite program. As an illustration, the baccalaureate degree has been an especially successful degree because it is flexible and accommodates many different majors. In a graduate program in educational administration, there could be one or at most two doctoral degrees, each providing for several different tracks leading to different career goals. Thus, one goal might be a career in research and teaching, another in central administration, and a third in staff administration. Each would require different experiences, but each presumably deals with a basic core of concepts, problems, approaches, and modes of thinking. A core curriculum of reasonable magnitude would seem to be an effective device; from such a core, individuals could develop quite flexible programs.

Heavy requirements, however, pose significant dangers. A required curriculum can become excessively rigid, as occurred in engineering and law curricula. It can, especially if concentrated in the first year, adversely affect student motivation by denying immediate and intensive entry into the desired specialization. It can penalize graduate students who must attend part-time because of work and economic considerations. It can, unless specific efforts are made to the contrary, appear to be irrelevant to the professional goals of some categories of students. And requirements can appear to students as simply hurdles to be overcome and barriers to the pursuit of what they believe to be the significant elements of their education.

The Curriculum: Applied or Theoretical?

A second major issue is whether the curriculum should emphasize application or theory. As of 1973, the faculty in administration, by virtue of training, experience, and inclination, ostensibly appeared to favor a theoretical valance. However, it collectively recognized the need to restore a heavier applied component. The quandary was how, how much, and through what agencies. Perhaps the issue can be most effectively examined through an analysis of such apparent techniques as dissertations, internships, field services, continuing education, relationships with the field of actual administrative practice, and the nature of various kinds of courses offered.

Ph.D. versus Ed.D.

The present state of entry into high-level educational administrative positions presents an unfortunate paradox. Increasingly, the doctorate, exemplified by the Ph.D. degree, is the expected credential yet it has historically been awarded for training and demonstrated competence to do original research. In an attempt to add balance, schools of education, including Stanford, created the Doctor of Education degree, which presumably prepared individuals to be practitioners. However, in the minds of many the Ed.D. degree was a second-class degree, since it did not stress the research component long presumed to be the hallmark of university graduate work. In institutions like Stanford, as the faculty became stronger in research competency and as it sought parity with other schools and departments in the university with respect to academic respectability, the form and to some extent the substance of the Ed.D. gradually came to resemble or even to be indistinguishable from the Ph.D. degree. Since the Ph.D. degree seemingly has higher prestige, a program that offers both the Ed.D. and Ph.D. ensures that students will opt for the Ph.D. degree even though in essence it does not represent the best preparation for students training for administrative roles. Essentially, what happens is that the form but not the substance of the traditional Ph.D. becomes the rule. In the School of Education at Stanford, this has produced several problems:

1. Many students in administration have no genuine desire to do a research-oriented dissertation. They view the Ph.D. as a necessary union card to become high-level administrators but they cannot really reconcile this ambition with the dissertation requirement.

2. The present course work for administration students is not really designed to prepare students for dissertation work, consisting, as it does, of a few courses in statistics and a smattering of other things. Students are required to take several introductory and workshop courses which do not prepare them to be economic or sociological scholars, nor are the courses ideally suited to prepare people for educational administration. The practice of administration is essentially eclectic, drawing on a number of concepts and disciplines to illuminate practical problems. The background for this is not ideal for preparing people to do research dissertations.

3. As a consequence, many students attempt to write dissertations in fields they have not studied extensively. They then face Hobson's choice: either they do more course work while conducting dissertation research to make up for gaps in their training, or they perform an inadequate, methodological exercise (frequently relying on consultative help to demonstrate procedures they don't understand).

4. Students are confused about faculty expectations and how to reconcile their own interests and goals with what they had come to believe were normal dissertation requirements. They would like to examine such things as the admissions practices of a given institution or a broad policy concern of a state agency, but feel they must be rigorously theoretical and make use of structured hypotheses and analysis of variance.

Few, if any, schools of education have resolved this problem. Most have compromised older standards as Stanford has; the Ph.D. is the more attractive degree but is essentially a weakened variant of the Ph.D. degree as interpreted in strong, disciplinary departments.

Again, several options are available. The first is to concentrate on the Ph.D., making it definitely a research degree requiring a great amount of disciplinary work. This undoubtedly would produce stronger dissertations, in the academic sense, but would likely be viewed as being even more irrelevant to the needs of future administrators than the present compromise. A second option is to continue the status quo, with mild fluctuations as to the nature of Ph.D. dissertations depending on the faculty in residence and the abilities of students to manipulate the system.

A third option is to revive the Ed.D. degree and to make it clearly a distinctive credential for future administrators. The best way to ensure distinctiveness would be to modify the dissertation requirements substantially. The Ed.D. dissertation could be an analysis (including relationships and insights of theory) of the implementation of a specific program, project, or policy. For example, a student might arrange for this implementation with a cooperating school district or other educational organization, and preferably would have major responsibility for the implementation phase. The dissertation document would then be a critical review of the administration of the project, stressing relationships of several theoretical concepts to actual practice. Students would be required to synthesize several of the theoretical strands in their program rather than deal in depth with any single strand, such as economics, sociology, or political science. Most applied situations require a fusion or an integration of disciplines rather than a single disciplinary analysis. There are, of course, dangers in this option. Theses based on a field experience can degenerate into superficial journalism or autobiography. It is possible for schools of education to drift into a posture of equating vocational experience with conceptual learning and offering academic credit and degrees to individuals merely for having survived in a job. And it is possible that a truly distinctive practitioner-oriented thesis would help perpetuate a presumed second-class citizen's status of schools of education. Still, the virtues are many, among them forcing a recognition that much of the proper work of schools of education is to prepare professional practitioners rather than to prepare incipient research scholars.

Field Experience

A related problem is that of providing field or clinical experience for students preparing for administrative careers. Most professional schools currently believe there should be a larger component of field experience in their curricula, yet to do so presents a number of complexities. There is considerable argument as to the advantages of an internship or field experience program.

Field experience has several potential advantages for students. It can offer a vital, real-life opportunity to integrate academic preparation with the professional demands of an actual situation, and it allows a balancing of the theoretical world of research with the world of practical experience. For example, in decision-making in a field setting the individual must evaluate alternatives and live with the results of decisions he makes. Some field experience can, of course, be simulated through special in-class projects or case studies, but simulation in this situation seems generally inferior to actual clinical or internship experience. In the field, the intern learns more or can learn more of the technical skills and processes of administration and can apply conceptual learnings to a work situation that would be impossible in virtually every other context. He can acquire intensive experience in certain administrative tasks and roles and he has the opportunity to observe extensively a wide variety of administrative situations. Further, fieldwork and internships can facilitate entry into an administrative career through the contacts and visibility that field experience allows. A not insignificant value of field experience is that, when remunerated (as it should be), students gain some assistance in bearing the heavy costs of graduate education. Further, a well-designed field or internship program can contribute to faculty growth. Close contact among university faculty members, their students, and practitioners can reduce the lag between the development of new knowledge, methodology, and media by administrative theorists and the implementation by practitioners. Professors supervising interns obtain field experiences that can challenge them to relate their knowledge to practical educational problems. As a consequence, they can be kept attuned to the developing needs of future educational administrators which can and should properly affect the university's own program and rectify its curricular deficiencies.

However, field or internship experiences are not without problems or difficulties. One problem is the extraordinarily high cost of a properly organized internship program. The internship has, of course, been most fully developed in schools of medicine, which offer the most expensive education of any of the professional fields. Internships require a considerable investment of faculty time as well as the time of supervisors in the host situation. Also, it is frequently difficult to persuade a host administrator to provide genuine learning experiences for an intern instead of routine tasks. There is a tendency for internships and field experiences to degenerate either into jobs taken primarily for economic reasons or into performance of routine and pedestrian tasks, often of a menial nature. And of course there is the danger that internships or field experiences off the campus may loosen ties with the academic program to such an extent that students stray from their academic programs in pursuit of further experience or more sustained funding.

Another important difficulty is locating enough appropriate positions into which students can be placed. One possible solution to this problem is a program of field services. A field services organization in a school of education is generally defined as a formal and recognized unit which seeks out and makes contractual arrangements between the school of education and other educational organizations for services to be performed by the faculty and students or other individuals possessing needed competencies. A comprehensive field services organization could provide the opportunity and places to train students in internships, and it offers sufficient variety to appeal to the varied interests and aspirations of students. At an earlier time at Stanford, there were several field services activities available to almost all students who wished to participate. Stanford graduates from that period have testified that their experiences in field services were among the most useful part of the program in preparing them for practice. A field services program articulated with the rest of the teaching and research in a school of education can facilitate relating theory to practice and serve as a conduit to transmit into the field the research and scholarly developments taking place in the university. Varied field activities can also promote greater liaison between practitioners and faculty and can contribute to enriched professional lives of each. And finally, a well-developed field services program could provide the setting in which more applied dissertations could be developed.

However, there are also counterarguments, several of a rather fundamental nature. The School of Education at Stanford considers itself to be a research school and most of the faculty are deeply involved in concentrated research. The question arises whether an active field service program is the best use of the time and talents of a faculty skilled in research techniques. Perhaps field-services activities should be undertaken by other institutions that do not rank research with such a high priority. In addition, Stanford is a private university whose resources come from tuition, endowment, and gifts and contracts, with the use of those funds frequently restricted to teaching or research purposes. If a field-services activity is not self-supporting from contracts, is the expenditure of institutional funds for services to other schools, colleges, or organizations defensible? A fundamental difference between state-supported institutions and private institutions is apparent here. State appropriations will frequently specify funds for continuing education, extension work, and field services. Schools of education in state-supported colleges can thus operate completely within their charters, which require service to the field. March addresses the essential issue as he ponders the role of the university in preparing administrators:

> Recent commentaries on administration, not only in education but also in business administration, military administration, and public administration, have emphasized the importance of three talents:
> (1) The talent to deal effectively with people;
> (2) The talent to manage conflict;
> (3) The talent to mediate between the organization and the broader society.
> Because of the importance of such talents, there have been suggestions that training programs for administration should include an amount of training time proportional to the importance of each talent. The suggestions depend on an implicit assumption that the talent return on training investment is constant across domains of training. The assumption seems implausible.
>
> The amount of time to be spent in a training program on different forms of training depends not only on the importance of the talent involved but also on the return (in terms of the value of talent improvement) per unit time spent in training. We have some ideas about how to improve the capabilities of administrators with respect to these three talents. However, the technologies are not well-developed; and some of them involve experiential teaching much more than the specification of formal knowledge or formal procedures. As a result, there is likely to be a relatively rapidly decreasing marginal return to time investment in training in some of these areas and a . . . compara-

tive disadvantage of educational institutions as the training grounds for such talents.

There are numerous areas of administrative training in which the university has an absolute advantage. . . . The list of domains in which the university has a simple advantage is long. Universities do as good a job as anyone in most aspects of management training. They do better in providing the basic knowledge and identifying general problems and isolating and providing broad experience in the necessary interpersonal and intellectual skills, in discussing value issues, and encouraging risk-taking and innovation, and building social and personal sensitivity, and exposure to conflicting ideas and sentiments, and at building a sense of self-esteem. . . .

Despite this, the university does not have a comparative advantage in all of these domains. It ought not to be a general purpose social institution, or even a general purpose participant in administrative training. The university has a special domain of competence: the domain of the intellect. What the university does best, relative to other institutions, is to develop new knowledge and its implications. It is an intellectual institution.

Except in a few areas of scholarly activity, universities are the site for the vast majority of the basic scholarship that is done in the United States. This is true throughout the biological, social, and physical sciences; in the humanities; and increasingly in the arts. It is true in almost every area of applied knowledge: law, medicine, engineering, education, business administration, criminology, social welfare, and politics.

In their history, universities have done other things. They have been linked with the religious establishment; they have managed major sports amusement systems; they have been centers for social experimentation in individual mores and social philosophy. But their primary claim is an intellectual one. Their faculties and students are smarter in intellectual terms and know more of the things that are learned in scholarly ways than most other people. They read, write, and think more and better than most other people. They have the time and the organization to do good research and good thinking.

Since the problems of the world are not necessarily amenable to intellectual solutions, the social value of a university can shift over time. With such a shift, we would expect some shift in the comparative advantage calculations also. Some nonintellectual activities would become more appropriate for the university. However, the shift in the problems of the world over time is almost certainly much greater than the shift in the comparative advantage of the university. Most of the time, regardless of the shifts in social needs, a university should retain the same basic specialization.

In a similar way, the advantage for university training in the training of administrators is primarily in the intellective domain. It is in providing the research basis for intelligence and in teaching the intellective skills of management. Other institutions are likely to have a comparative advantage in other training areas. As the mix of administrative needs shifts, the university's primary role is to provide the intellectual base of new skills; it is not to attempt to provide all of the training. For some administrative jobs and some administrators, the university is a relatively inefficient training center. Some important administrative tasks have relatively small intellectual components. It may be considerably more vital that the administrator be strong, or loving, or energetic, or sensitive, or charismatic, or a member of a particular social, ethnic, or sexual group. We can recognize the importance of such tasks and the legitimacy and value of such attributes without accepting the proposition that the university should provide either the training or the certification for them.[1]

Implied in the issue of field services is the relationship between the administrative program at Stanford and the local communities. But the matter seems larger than that and in a way exposes and elaborates one of the major changed conditions of American higher education. During much of the history of American colleges and universities they could exist and function relatively effectively in isolation.

However, as institutions grew larger, recruited a more heterogenous student body, and consumed larger proportions of available capital, they increasingly impinged on and interreacted with their surrounding communities. Many of the troublesome episodes of the 1960s, beginning with the free speech movement in Berkeley, through the crisis at Columbia, and culminating tragically at Kent State, were brought about by the encounter between educational institutions and their immediate constituencies and the surrounding environment. As the administration faculty sought to fashion its future, it had to address this matter of relationships and involvement or noninvolvement with its surrounding community. Barbara Hatton eloquently analyzes the issue and urges a definite position:

> If we are realistically to pursue our stated goals of preparing practicing educational administrators and administrative analysts, then we must develop some way to have these potential leaders understand intellectually the realities of the local school environments, purposes, structures, and people living within these. Similarly, local schools and communities are facing dramatic environmental changes which preclude unmediated or misused knowledge for appropriate institutional response. Nothing seems more timely or potentially beneficial to both parties then the forging of a "learned consortia" designed to undertake the specialized tasks for which our students are to be trained and to undertake the tasks which are required by situations in local schools and communities. If our programmatic necessity is viewed in the context of the dramatic environmental changes which are confronting local schools and communities today, the message seems clear: Our administrative faculty must ... get back into the business of "university/community relations." The remaining questions are simply how, how much, and what kind.
>
> I believe that, rather than supporting the increasing tendency here (at both the doctoral and master's level) to ignore the day-to-day conduct of local schools and the processes which affect them, the professional preparation interests as well as the research and development interests of the unique group we have assembled would better be served by first strengthening the concept of an educational

"ecosystem" within our group: . . . local schools and communities become a part of an "ecosystem" that constitutes the total academic environment. Necessary but different kinds of learning are assumed to come from each agency and constituent that affect educational processes and organizations. The embodiment of such a concept as related to our goal of preparation of administrative leadership might be found in the development of a matrix of experiences wherein each faculty member and student, regardless of academic specialty, would have the opportunity for the integration of research and application, of scholarship and dissemination. Broad incentives that encourage each student to seek such integration, especially in local school arenas, are probably needed. They can and should be provided.

. . . What I have in mind is that we conceive of ourselves as nothing less than a RAND Corporation in spirit where each person possesses or attempts to gain possession of certain skills applicable to the local school arena as well as any other particular clientele of professional interests. I am not advocating that the administration program be transformed into a prep school for public school superintendents (or administrators) so that each graduate might be prepared to serve in such a capacity should the opportunity arise, but there should be opportunity for choice of clientele on the part of the student (this choice does not effectively exist in our program as presently operated). And more importantly, such an opportunity is essential to our goal of producing men and women who can provide high-quality leadership in educational organizations. Such men and women can only be produced if they are required to use specialized research and administrative skills in selective endeavors whose large and generous nature permit synthesis of academic experiences. We should strive toward complete interaction of student and educational systems. To omit any agency or level is to construct an unreal wall between student and academic experience. To provide interaction with one educational agency or constituent to the exclusion of all others is to construct an unreal environment for academic experience.

We must somehow accomplish involvement with local schools and communities. We have no effective involvement at this point in our programmatic operations and there are compelling reasons immediately to seek such involvement. A few of these reasons bear specific delineation:

1. Educational administration as a field represents a borrowing or redirecting of literature from seemingly pertinent material in other fields which is largely untested in the local school arena. Programmatic involvement with local schools and communities can provide an opportunity for judging the potential for affecting the educational environment from gleaning insights into the function, practices, and contexts of local school administration. Such a developmental step would be significant in the field of educational administration.

2. The development of a model of cooperative arrangements of university groups with school systems and groups could provide maximum opportunities for all parties mutually concerned with particular educational problems to maximize currently available resources in approaching them. Such an approach should have higher yield for students, faculty, and cooperating schools than the individual consulting arrangements which now prevail. Our experiences with local schools and communities could contribute to the development of such a model.

3. Effective preparation of educational administrators and leaders requires a conceptualization of the total educational enterprise of which local school settings are an integral part. Such preparation requires an ecological approach to administrative preparation in which involvement with local school settings can achieve contextual meaning.

4. If there is an esprit de corps in our present administrative faculty, it is so subtle as to be indiscernible. Some collective endeavor might contribute to a feeling of fellowship or some sense of community within our group. An area commitment to pursue relations with local communities could serve such a function.

5. The problems and prospects of local schools and local school communities must be approached with a larger vision of organization and of the world which the administrative faculty has a unique capacity to provide.

6. It is immoral by some standards to purport provision of preparation for practicing leadership in local school settings while ignoring experience with local school settings as an integral part of the student's preparation. We absorb the top intellectual ability from within local school settings and their children. While their training presents some challenge to nearby school districts, involvement with local communities could provide some moral identity for our program.

7. The rejection of the panacea approach to educational reform supports and enhances the promise for development of models for change and program planning appropriate to the local school context. As in any developmental enterprise, actual involvement is required at some level.

8. . . . We can no longer afford to indulge ourselves in our current contempt for practitioners, especially those in the local arena, lest we sacrifice our ability to provide competent educational leadership. The only obstacle that prevents us from realistic relationships with local communities is our loyalty to a concept of "pure" academic training that will soon make our programs obsolete to those concerned with practicing administrative leadership.[2]

Much of the literature about innovation and reform in professional education advocates more and more intense relationships between professional schools and other units of the university. One of the historic arguments for lodging schools within a single university structure is to facilitate interaction. It is assumed that the students of medicine gain a great deal from interacting with professors and students in the basic sciences, and that law students can profit from rubbing intellectual elbows with those who will be social workers. Particularly in a small professional school like the School of Education at Stanford, which has a limited number of faculty positions, adequately rich educational programs can only be offered if resources from elsewhere in the university are available. This point may be illustrated by considering the subspecialty of higher education. For almost twenty-five years, the Stanford School of Education has maintained a program in higher education which has been highly productive of individuals moving into reasonably high-level administrative positions. During most of that time, there was only one professor in the school primarily concerned with higher education. Such one-man departments have been severely criticized by accreditation agencies and critics of higher education; the Stanford program would have been exceedingly vulnerable to criticism or even sanction had not there been ways by which other resources could be placed at the disposal of students. But for the most part those relationships have been casual and quite personal, depending on the style or inclination of the incumbent in the higher educational role. Assuming that a strong case can be made for close relationships between the administration program and other parts of the university, as being essential to the content of the administrative program, the question becomes, How can the previously casual and personal techniques be institutionalized so that students can generally expect in one way or another sustained exposure outside the professional school of education?

Professor Henry Levin analyzes this question and suggests some of the conditions that must be met if the goal of interschool and interdepartmental cooperation is to be achieved:

> Cooperation between two schools of a university takes place when certain conditions are satisfied. Although the academic argument can be made that joint activities will take place when there is an overlap in academic concerns, I do not believe that this is actually the case. Experience has shown that the different academic divisions of universities would much prefer to operate within real or imagined jurisdictional boundaries rather than to sanctify commonalities with joint participation. I believe that there exist three principles that underlie joint programs between schools of the university: (1) a common interest in developing programs in areas that are not yet serviced; (2) the possibility of substantial cost savings or program enhancement by sharing student and faculty resources; and (3) the provision of financial incentives from University or external sources that will be allocated to co-operative programs. To

these one could add the nonvoluntary principle of coercion as well, but I am assuming that the University will not use such a lever to effect joint ventures among schools or departments.

As new areas of employment and research demand arise, these will be reflected in pressures on the University to construct programs that respond to these demands. In some cases the focus of such programs can be satisfied within the traditional departmental or school context of the University, but in other cases there appears to be an intersection of jurisdictions reflected in the emerging area. In the latter case, specific units of the University may feel inadequate to address new programs in the area or may feel that they will benefit through cooperation with other units of the university. Questions of credibility and jurisdictional conflicts may also be at issue if a School attempts to construct new programs in areas which clearly overlap with the ostensible responsibilities of other Schools of the University.

Under these circumstances it will often be beneficial for two schools to cooperate in planning programs of joint interest and in implementing them. A case in point is the projected law and education program, which grew out of the increasing public and scholarly activities represented by the intersection of these phenomena in the everyday world. Increasingly the courts are being used to challenge the methods of financing education, to desegregate the schools, to define and protect students' rights, and so on. Individual faculty members of the School of Education and the School of Law were encountering increasingly problems which could not be analyzed with the relatively narrow confines of their profession, so informal consultation and discussion between members of the two faculties took place in order to exchange ideas and wisdom. At the same time an increasing number of students in both schools expressed interest in studying the relationships between law and education. Finally, the governmental and private foundations began to show an interest in promoting programs that intersect the two areas. The result of these events was an interest in the law and education. As new phenomena arise that bridge the space between the field of education and other fields, we can expect a corresponding interest in bridging the training and research gap across the appropriate Schools of the University.

Somewhat related to the first principle is the incentive to share resources for existing programs or ones that are newly implemented in one of the schools of the University. For example, as the School of Education began increasingly to pursue a heavier social science and statistical input into its programs, it considered purchasing the time of faculty in related departments. In a few cases successful arrangements were worked out. In other cases courtesy appointments were arranged to increase the credibility of our social science offerings on the one hand while adding to the faculty resources of the co-operating departments and schools on the other. In these cases there was a mutual interest in sharing resources for either cost-saving or program enhancement purposes.

Similarly, to the degree that students can take some of their course-work in other departments, the resources of other parts of the university can be brought to bear on the education of our students. Even if there is a requisite *quid pro quo* in our enrolling and advising students from other schools and departments, the net effect is to increase the richness of student experiences in cooperating schools. To a certain degree these types of relationships prevail between the psychology and sociology departments and the School of Education, where relatively large numbers of students move across departmental boundaries. Interdepartmental representation on program committees is a further example of the cost savings or program enhancement motive.

While related to the previous categories, it is important to consider as a special case the provision of financial incentives to create joint programs. That is, the stirrings of joint activity in research and employment domains are rarely adequate in themselves for separate jurisdictions of a university to consider overcoming the traditional inertia that stands in the path of joint venture among schools. Foundations and government agencies have responded by offering financial resources for certain types of cooperative programs. Our ill-fated joint program with the Graduate School of Business is a good example of an intersection created primarily by financial incentives.

The most important characteristic of the cooperation created by external financial support is its fragility when the support evaporates. Although it is possible that such a financial inducement is given in order to "prime the pump," . . . the pump tends to break down when the priming stops. The important lesson to be learned . . . is the need to build strong ties and incentives to continue the cooperation when the funding terminates or to guarantee funding indefinitely. The damage that can occur from canceling programs that were glued together primarily by financial bonds may be greater in the long run than the short-run gains of cooperation. Thus we should be aware of the basis for joint cooperation and the probability of its continuation when external support disappears.

. . . More specifically, I can think of eight types of joint relations, each representing a different degree of involvement and commitment:

1. Informal cooperation among faculty and among students on matters of joint interest;
2. Interdepartmental and interschool enrollments of students;
3. Interdepartmental and interschool school student advisement (e.g., thesis and advisory committees);
4. Courtesy faculty appointments with other schools and departments;
5. Jointly sponsored courses;
6. Joint faculty appointments;
7. Joint research endeavors of a formal nature;
8. Joint instructional programs;
9. Joint degree programs.

While these categories are not meant to be strictly hierarchal, there is a general tendency to move from limited involvement at the top of the list to complete cooperative

immersion at the bottom. Depending on the particular
joint concerns that arise between the administrative faculty and other units of the university, different combinations of these activities might be appropriate.

Resolution of one issue conditions virtually all other matters: the
role of the school of education in a high-cost, selective, private university. When Stanford began to offer professional education, it had
just recently ended its status as a free tuition school but was still
sufficiently inexpensive (particularly in view of lenient loan arrangements for tuition) so that those wishing to enter education could still
economically do so. During much of the early twentieth century the
School of Education produced many of the teachers, principals, and
superintendents who manned California's public schools. However,
conditions began to change rapidly, particularly after World War II.
The state teachers colleges expanded their programs in many fields,
especially in the liberal arts and sciences and developed professional
programs that were competitive with those offered by Stanford. The
University of California expanded from its Berkeley-Davis-UCLA
base to its present eight general campus structure and competed seriously with Stanford in fields ranging from preparation of teachers for
vocational educational programs to preparation of junior college
leaders. At the same time, the School of Education at Stanford, moving in concert with other parts of the university, began a radical shift
in emphasis toward research and scholarship. Teaching loads
dropped, service commitments were minimized, and external funding
for research and research-related contracts expanded enormously. As
a first indication of change, the School of Education eliminated its
small but effective program for the preparation of elementary school
teachers. Then, as departments in the School of Humanities and Sciences began to eliminate the master's degree or to regard it primarily
as a consolation prize, Stanford's role in the preparation of junior
college teachers deteriorated; by the late 1960s only a handful of students in English were being explicitly prepared for junior college
teaching. As the research preoccupation of the university as a whole
grew, administrative officials came to view some of the service activities of the School of Education, such as the School Facilities Planning Laboratory, the field services unit, and the summer session, as
perhaps inappropriate for a professional school in a private univer-

sity. The School of Education continued to prepare secondary school teachers though in relatively small numbers, motivated at least in part to provide laboratory situations and materials for the federally financed research and development center for teaching. In the field of administration, Stanford no longer prepared its proportional share of individuals who would serve as presidents of junior colleges, superintendents of school districts, and school principals. Public school systems and public junior colleges increasingly turned to the larger suppliers of professional personnel at the University of California at Berkeley, the University of California at Los Angeles, and the University of Southern California. There was not a complete moratorium concerning such appointments, but nonetheless the shift was perceptible. For example, out of eighty-six doctoral recipients who graduated between 1968 and 1973, twenty-five had positions in elementary and secondary administration, thirty-seven had positions in higher education, but only five in junior college administration. Twelve held appointments with government research institutes or for private firms, and for twelve others no record was available on where they were employed. The graduates now serving in governmental agencies, bureaucracies, and the like are probably indicative of where Stanford graduates are going; they include: NIE research grant officer, U.S. Office of Education; vice-president of McGraw-Hill; research scholar, College Entrance Examination Board; U.S. Air Force educational consultant; and chief of the Drug Education Unit of the California State Department of Education.

Options for the Future

As the faculty in administration of the School of Education charts its future, several options seem reasonably open, although they are always conditioned by developments in the rest of the School of Education and the university. One option would be to concentrate even more on research, accepting as students only those individuals with potential research talent who could be supported by external research funding. This implies a very small student body, possibly consisting of half postdoctoral students and half doctoral students who anticipate becoming the professors of educational administration for the next generation. Such a development would probably be consistent with the activities and quite possibly the interests of the present faculty, but would tend to cut the school off from actual field practice in administration even more than is presently true. In addition, since research activities would be dependent on external funding, considerable variation in research emphases would be inevitable as interests of sources of research funds shifted over time. At the other extreme, the faculty in administration could again seek to prepare school principals and administrators through modifying its program in the direction of much more applied materials. This would of course run counter to the interests of many of the present faculty, although over time those interests could change, especially if new appointments to the faculty were made directly from active school situations. However, this would intensify competition between Stanford and publicly supported colleges and universities, which are able to offer similar training programs at considerably less cost. This matter can be starkly stated: What can Stanford possibly do to prepare public school principals better to be worth the difference in tuition of almost $3,200 a year at Stanford and $360 a year at the University of California at Berkeley? Assuming that Stanford and the School of Education intend to maintain a presence in educational administration (an assumption by no means unquestionable), some middle ground must be found that could conceivably produce in relatively small but equivalent numbers, individuals entering mainstream administrative or managerial posts, individuals headed toward staff positions in the various bureaucracies, individuals to become professors and scholars, and, possibly through the School of Education's emphasis on international education, individuals from foreign countries who would become educational leaders in their own countries. It is conceivable that these kinds of individuals could receive a substantively superior preparation, in part because relationships with other professional fields at Stanford might be somewhat better than is generally the case, hence programs could reflect the relevance of legal, business, or even engineering educations.

The choices open to an administration faculty in a private university must be considered in light of problems of enrollment. The faculty does not have the luxury of simply deciding which program emphasis it wishes to pursue and the precise numbers of students it will accept. Several constraints operate forcibly. The School of Education has traditionally enrolled a fairly stable number of students, although there was a noticeable drop after the mid 1960s. Were the school to restrict enrollments precipitously, this would raise questions that would impinge on the number of faculty, the support provided the school from university funds, and comparison with other schools and departments in the university. Secondly, there is a critical mass constraint. If a program is to have enough visibility to attract students, to attract the interests of prospective employers, and to attract funding, it must be of sufficient size and the faculty must reflect sufficient variety of interests. This critical mass constraint would mitigate against the enrollments implied if the faculty were to become preoccupied with research and preparing research scholars. Thirdly, there is the constraint imposed by the decreasing demand for educational workers. There is a serious oversupply of Ph.D. recipients in most of the arts and sciences, and in the relatively near future there is likely to be an oversupply of doctoral recipients prepared to administer schools, colleges, and systems of schools and colleges. A high-cost institution such as Stanford must be extraordinarily conscious of the need to place graduates in positions of sufficiently high potential to warrant the charges that Stanford must levy. A fourth constraint is the number of faculty available for the program in administration. There are or will be approximately six full-time-equivalent faculty members for administration comprised of approximately nine individuals. As Stanford University approaches a steady state, few if any additions to the faculty in any of the schools or departments are likely to be approved. While many large universities have heavy doctoral student enrollment per faculty member, there is serious question that doctoral work in its best sense can be offered under such conditions. Many other schools of education conduct undergraduate programs that provide large enough enrollments to justify larger faculties. The School of Education at Stanford is exclusively a graduate institution, emphasizing primarily doctoral-level work. The dilemma which all of this produces can be bluntly stated: The faculty in administration must enroll enough students to make the program economically viable, yet to do so may dilute the quality of the educational effort sufficiently to eliminate any distinctions that might make the high cost of attending Stanford desirable to prospective students. That equation is further complicated by the fact that the university, the School of Education, and the faculty in administration, stress affirmative action on minority students and women, a factor with many complications ranging from purely fiscal to the composition of whatever critical mass of students is finally adopted as optimum.

The enrollment issue, as well as the more fundamental issue of the viability of the program in administration at Stanford, will be resolved, if it *is* resolved, to the degree that the program can be innovative, economical, and distinctive. In expansive times, innovativeness and distinctiveness could be purchased with readily available funds for new programs, but in a more stagnant situation the direct purchase option is not available. There is no panacea, but it is apparent that there must be major changes in the way things are done. The Carnegie Commission on Higher Education contends that institutional and program renewal will require considerable self-discipline in a number of areas:

> Self-discipline at the institutional level can be aided by:
>
> (1) *Improving the budget-making process.* We suggest that the budget assign total costs to each endeavor (including rentals for space and equipment—there is little incentive to save on what are "free" goods); that it consolidate consideration of capital and operating budgets so that the impact of each on the other can better be seen and trade-offs can be made—for example, in considering year-round operations; that it look at the long-term and not just the individual year; that it concentrate more on outputs and less exclusively on inputs, and particularly more on "value added."
>
> (2) *Obtaining better data and making it more widely available within the academic community.* It is particularly important to have (a) global cost and output data among institutions of comparable quality and with comparable endeavors and (b) specific cost and output data among departments within the same institution. Quality is of the essence in academic life and it is hard to measure; but among carefully selected institutions and within the same institution it may be assumed to be sufficiently equal so that comparisons can be made—it is easier to compare quality than it is to measure it. But even within these restricted limits great care must be taken in making comparisons; they are a starting point but not the end point of proper

consideration. The best measure of output is student credit hours—for example, student credit hours per $1,000. "Data pools" can be helpful—like the ACE studies of quality at the graduate level. Regional associations also can be helpful in creating them and some, in particular the SREB in the South and WICHE in the West, are. The U.S. Office of Education has a particular responsibility in regard to cost and output data. Consortia, as among certain private colleges in Pennsylvania, can also be helpful in gathering and exchanging data.

The information system is now very poor in higher education.

(3) *Maximizing flexibility in creation of space and in making commitments to people.* This assists the process of necessary change. New projects should be on a trial basis; faculty members with tenure should be a reasonable proportion of the total instructional staff; early retirement on a part-time or full-time basis should be possible; young faculty members should be hired with regard to their adaptability to future assignments—the young faculty members hired in 1972 will retire in the year 2012; certain of the positions vacated should be recaptured for central reassignment; and so forth.

(4) *Setting a quota of "liberated" money each year, as suggested above, perhaps 1 to 3 percent.* This money, taken from old assignments either on an across-the-board or selective basis, can then be used for reform, for new projects, for meeting the more volatile career and academic interests of students. Some old activities should be stopped altogether.

(5) *Having a competent central staff with adequate authority.*

(6) *Creating incentives to save.* The state can share savings with the campus rather than demand them all and thus make them disappear. The faculty can be assured benefits from savings, for example, some proportion might be assigned to salary increases or library purchases; and also the students—for example, more money for student aid or lower tuition increases. Faculty and students will need to

share in some advisory role in budget making for these incentives to be fully effective.

The only way to keep faculty salaries ahead of the cost of living, to improve the library, to get more money for scholarships, to keep down increases in tuition, to get academic reform may be to make other adjustments in resource use. Hard choices must be made. Incentives can help both in making them and gaining their acceptance.

(7) *Convincing the faculty of the need to be more cost-conscious.* The severity of the new situation is not as yet always fully appreciated. The 1960s were an unusual period; not par for the academic course. Salaries cannot keep rising so fast on a comparative basis; teaching loads may have to be increased instead of reduced; facilities and amenities cannot be so significantly improved; new Ph.D. programs cannot so readily be added.

For many institutions survival is at stake; for all, a confrontation with public support already exists.

But only so much can be done. One rule is that it is easier to manage things in academic life, than people—to save on things, to centralize control of their use. Another rule is that effective use of resources is a political as well as a technical problem. From a political point of view, outside pressure helps—from the market or from the state budget authority provided it is reasonable in amount and general in form. Across-the-board cuts are easier than selective cuts. Cuts are best offset by some generalized gains for the participants. Consultants can ease action by taking responsibility for difficult recommendations. Good data, widely distributed, are essential. People should not be taken by surprise—consultation and hearings are a part of the educational process. The economies of the situation can only be handled well as the politics are conducted with care and consideration."[3]

It was in a serious effort to resolve some of these issues that the faculty in administration of the School of Education at Stanford conducted an intensive planning exercise during the summer of 1973. Succeeding chapters examine how the faculty proceeded and the resolution of the various issues.

Notes

1. James G. March, "Analytical Skills and the University Training of Educational Administrators," Seventh Annual Walter Cocking Memorial Lecture, Bellingham, Wash., 1973.

2. Barbara R. Hatton, "Realistic Relations with Local Communities," unpublished manuscript, July 30, 1973.

3. Carnegie Commission on Higher Education, *The More Effective Use of Resources* (New York: McGraw-Hill, June 1972), § 18, pp. 23-24. (Reprinted by permission.)

3. Rationale for a Program

The New Graduate Program in Education

The process of deep immersion in curriculum construction of the faculty in administration at the Stanford School of Education produced a remarkable consensus. The faculty agreed that there should be a relatively small, highly selective, and focused program in administration allowing for three emphases or subconcentrations (elementary and secondary education, higher education, and policy analysis). There will be three degree options: a master of arts, an Ed.D., and a Ph.D., the anticipation being that the largest enrollments will be in the master's and Ed.D. programs. Approximately 80 percent of doctoral candidates will probably opt for the Ed.D., which program will be clearly and distinctively organized to suit the needs of practitioners. The first year of what is intended to be essentially a full-time residential program will be largely prescribed for all students regardless of degree goal. The core of prescribed courses will consist of three year-long sequences: one in decision science, with a substantial mathematics and computer component; a second elaborating the social scientific bases of administration; and a third developing the nature of educational institutions and the modes by which they are organized, governed, and administered. All students are to be encouraged or required to take considerable course work outside the School of Education. All Ed.D. candidates will be required to take a supervised internship closely linked to a colloquium offered in conjunction with the internship, which normally will fall in the second year of the program. All Ph.D. candidates will be required to possess reasonably sophisticated statistical understanding and, in addition, to have demonstrated the research and analytical skills in one of the relevant social and behavioral sciences that are normally developed by Ph.D. candidates in those disciplines. The Ed.D. dissertation will be definitely of an applied sort with a wide range of approaches and topics possible. The Ph.D. dissertation will be clearly a research dissertation, representing a publishable contribution to knowledge. Admission to any of the programs will be based primarily on demonstrated intellectual and academic traits and achievement, although clearly relevant work experience may be included in the admission equation. This small program, typically enrolling no more than fifty or sixty students at one time in all phases of the program, will be supported financially through direct budget support from the university, although when possible external support for such things as research or intern traineeships will be used. Through a deliberate policy of opening professional courses in administration to enrollment from other units of the university, it is hoped that course enrollments may be kept at reasonable levels. For most courses, the mode will be easy access by advanced undergraduates from Stanford coupled with rigorous intellectual demands in the courses themselves.

The Issues

As the faculty undertook its task it faced most of the issues that confront professional education and education for the professions generally, as well as a number of issues that were indigenous to Stanford or comparable private and high quality institutions. The first issue was simply whether or not a high-cost, private, research-oriented university should maintain a professional school of education and a program designed to prepare educational administrators. The expansion of the capacity to prepare educational workers on the part of publicly supported institutions during the 1950s and 1960s was of such magnitude that those institutions alone presumably could supply the needed educational manpower throughout the rest of the twentieth century. Since they were largely supported by state appropriations, tuitions or fees were naturally lower than those a private institution had to charge. Unless a program in a private university was demonstrably and qualitatively different from programs maintained by public institutions, private institutions would be at a serious competitive disadvantage. Some have argued that the very nature of professional education was such that qualitative differences were difficult if not impossible to maintain. Prospective teachers needed to learn something of the history and functioning of educational institutions, something of the developmental needs of students at each of various educational levels, something of the range of pedagogical techniques and devices available, and to have been socialized to some extent to the role of teacher through practice teaching experience. Similarly, aspirant administrators needed to know some of the legal and financial bases of educational institutions, some techniques and strategies for supervising professional workers, how data could be used to affect decisions, and some knowledge and understanding of the role of administrator in a complex educational bureaucracy. Presumably these could be as well developed in the lower-cost public institutions as in the more expensive privately supported universities.

The decision for Stanford to maintain a strong posture in professional education was made earlier by the university and by the School of Education itself, which had conducted a study of its own future during the academic year 1971-72. The reasons were manyfold. First was the long tradition of Stanford leadership in professional education, illustrated by such contributions as those of Terman in the measurement of intelligence and the study of the gifted, Cubberley in the science and practice of school administration, Sears in the psychology of learning, and Cowley in the scholarly examination of the nature of higher education. Secondly, private universities aspire to contribute very high numbers of individuals to leadership roles in the society, and as education has evolved as one of the pivotal institutions in American society, the failure to contribute leadership through education would forfeit a major arena of influence. Thirdly, although publicly supported and privately supported universities increasingly tend to resemble each other as quasi public utilities, there are still qualitative differences between them. Private institutions are usually freer from direct political oversight and bureaucratic control external to the institution, hence they are somewhat freer to innovate and redeploy resources quickly in response to changing conditions. Especially with respect to education, in which profound changes were taking place, it seemed desirable that there should be some institutions that would be deliberately innovative, emphasizing the quest for new and frequently unorthodox knowledge. Although the opposite decision could have been made, the decision was to maintain the School of Education with a large number of tenured faculty and charged with a major research responsibility, coupled with the responsibility to prepare a limited number of individuals who, it was hoped, would develop into key leaders in education.

The decision to maintain a strong position in educational administration derived directly from those same considerations. The faculty appointed to administration were for the most part prepared as research scholars in one or several of the relevant academic disciplines such as history, economics, political science, or sociology. It was believed if the insights, talents, and interests of such a faculty could be judiciously blended with sophisticated awareness of the needs of actual educational administrative practice, the result could be conducive to the training of a small number of people who possibly could become agents of important educational change. The faculty was aware that in the past small groups of individuals working together have been disproportionately influential in modifying attitudes or conditions in the society. The work of a small cadre of scholars at the University of Chicago in the late 1920s and early 1930s to the study of administration of higher education is one example: Ralph W. Tyler, John Dale Russell, A. J. Brumbaugh, Floyd W. Reeves, and a small group of students made seminal contributions to the understanding of educational objectives and the finance and administration of collegiate institutions. Whether or not the faculty in administration at Stanford and their students can become a significant critical mass for change of course has yet to be demonstrated. However, the quest seems worthwhile and the program plan was designed to facilitate it.

Program Size

In light of this rationale, the first operational decision had to do with program size and emphasis. The fact that there was a serious oversupply of credentialed educational administrators suggested that numbers should be kept small. This was reinforced by the existence of a small faculty with no expectation of a marked increase in the number of faculty appointed to administration. Stanford University has adopted a policy of achieving a steady state, permitting perhaps 1½ to 2 percent annual growth to accommodate growth and changes in the intellectual fields of concern to the university. Thus, no discipline or professional field can expect to exceed those rates, except occasionally. The faculty in administration contains eight individuals who, because of other obligations held by some of them, are equivalent to approximately six full-time faculty. Adequate guidance and close supervision of dissertation or internship work is possible only if each full-time faculty member is responsible for not more than three or four doctoral recipients each year; an ideal arrangement would be no more than one or two doctoral recipients each year. Such numbers allow for the long hours of consultation and discussion that scholarly work requires. An exclusively graduate professional school is in a vulnerable position when it adheres to such small numbers, since it does not offer large undergraduate courses whose enrollments generate the necessary tuition income to offset the small graduate seminars and the tutorial work involved in thesis supervision. This may be alleviated in several ways. A strong master's degree can be provided, which makes no presumption as to developing a research competency in recipients; thus the numbers of master's candidates can be allowed to expand somewhat, if there is a real demand for the degree. Experience after the mid-1960s suggested that there was such a demand and that it could be accommodated. Secondly, particularly since the mid-1960s, both undergraduate students and students in other professional fields appear to have become intensely interested in education and educational concerns and problems. Assuming that such interest continues, courses in a professional field could be so organized as to serve both the professional needs of graduate students in education and the liberal or contextual educational needs of other students. This development can be facilitated by modifying the course numbering system, which in most institutions has been of only symbolic value, so that advanced undergraduates and graduate students in other fields can enroll in education courses. Substantial modification or elimination of prerequisites is also required, on the ground that they typically are nonfunctional. These two decisions can be made without compromising intellectual rigor within the courses themselves. This should result in larger course enrollments to provide offsets for the limited number of matriculants in doctoral programs. Obviously, additional financial support will be continuously sought as the faculty pursues its research or service mission; however, no reliance is placed on providing significant support for major components of the program from external and temporary funding. Essentially, the intention is to offer a relatively expensive doctoral program to a limited number of students (expense modified somewhat through larger course enrollments) as an educational responsibility of a privately supported and endowed university.

Program Emphases

Related to size is the matter of subconcentrations or emphases. A program in administration can be envisioned that would have specific strengths and program concentrations in such specialties as school facilities planning, principalships, institutional research, junior college administration, student personnel work, curriculum supervision, budget analysts, directors of admissions or administration of private, elementary, or secondary schools. The Stanford faculty in administration rejected the concept of comprehensive coverage and representation of a large number of specialties, partly because it was unattainable (given the small faculty), and more importantly because it did not appear to be especially desirable. It was assumed that many specializations of practice are best developed after entry into a job. While administering a parochial school system differs in many respects from administering a public school system, and presiding over a junior college differs from presiding over a complex university, the differential skills derive from a common body of understandings, principles, techniques, strategies, and rhetoric. The decision was made to offer only three subconcentrations or emphases, each of which would be broadly based allowing individuals subsequently to move in any of a number of different professional directions. The three selected were elementary and secondary school administration, higher education, and "policy analysis." This last was based on the assumption that, as educational structures become more complicated, there is increasing need for personnel to weigh policy alternatives and to develop strategies for implementation of policy; this kind of activity seemed to require a somewhat different preparation than that of individuals aspiring to occupy central administrative or management roles. Because the first year of the program in administration is largely prescribed, students will choose which of the three he wishes to emphasize during the second, third, and, in the case of Ph.D.s, fourth year of their graduate study. Master's candidates can, of course, adapt their specific interests through the one quarter of their program which is elective, or through extending the time of their master's programs by taking summer work either before or after the full year of residency.

Stanford, like most universities maintaining schools of education, has struggled with the problem of contriving a doctoral degree suitable to practicing administrators. Although the tendency might be decried, increasingly the doctorate has come to be the expected credential for professional practice (e.g., witness the change in law degrees from the bachelor to the doctoral designation). The Ed.D. degree, combined in some institutions with a subdoctoral educational specialist degree, has been emphasized as the proper preparation for practitioners. However, there has typically been an unfortunate regression of Ed.D. programs toward the form if not the substance of Ph.D. programs, caused by the presumed higher regard in which the Ph.D. is held, which is in turn largely due to the hegemony in universities of graduate faculties in arts and sciences. Yet a regressed Ed.D. degree can never be exactly comparable to the Ph.D., if the presumed needs of practicing administrators are accommodated. The result is that Ed.D. candidates have been forced to overcome hurdles largely irrelevant to their professional futures and to contrive dissertations that resemble Ph.D. theses but for which the candidates have been inadequately prepared. At Stanford, this process was intensified when several requirements for the Ph.D. were dropped. Before 1968, the larger number of candidates at Stanford sought and received the Ed.D. degree. In that year the language requirement for the Ph.D. was eliminated as a university requirement and the School of Education decided not to retain it. Almost immediately, any candidate who had earned a master's degree outside of education opted for the Ph.D., since his master's degree could stand in lieu of the only remaining distinction between the two degrees, which was a minor outside the School of Education. However, most of the Ph.D. candidates were not prepared in a disciplinary sense to do dissertations comparable in sophistication to those done by their counterparts in the arts and sciences departments. What were being produced were really hybrids, possessing some of the characteristics of Ed.D. candidates and some of Ph.D. candidates but with the surviving traits being the more lethal rather than the more beneficial. One way out of this dilemma would of course be to eliminate the Ed.D. degree and to impose requirements for the Ph.D. that would be comparable to those in force in the various departments in the arts or sciences. This alternative had considerable appeal for a disciplinary-prepared faculty, but did not accommodate the interests or needs of the large majority of applicants to the School of Education. Pursuing the opposite alternative of offering only the Ed.D. degree also seemed unwise because it would minimize the contributions that the faculty could make and would eliminate an important segment of professional workers—those who aspire to research roles and roles of professors in schools of education. A compromise seemed possible, that is, to offer both the Ed.D. and the Ph.D. degrees but to make them clearly distinctive. Although there is some reality to the presumed difference in prestige between the Ed.D. degree and the Ph.D. degree, in education this has not been reflected in differences in subsequent professional status or rewards. The task was to tailor the Ed.D. degree so that it would be clearly desirable for many students, especially those aspiring to administrative positions. This is to be contrived first through making the Ed.D. degree the principal degree offered. Any possible invidious distinction between Ph.D. and Ed.D. candidates would be offset by the larger number of students in the latter program. Secondly, Ed.D. candidates would be relieved from doing dissertation proposals in the Ph.D. mode, which requires theoretical and analytical skills that they do not have. Rather, dissertations would be applied, requiring students to synthesize a variety of concepts, theories, and evidence in solving applied problems. Previously, a dissertation examining the admissions policies of the Claremont group of colleges in the light of changing national admissions policies, leading to specific recommendations, would have been an unacceptable Ph.D. thesis. However, such an inquiry, well designed and rigorously conducted, would be highly appropriate for the Ed.D. program. Thirdly, a paid internship is an integral part of the Ed.D. curriculum and offers, in addition to the experiential values, some financial assistance for the second year of graduate study. Fourthly, the Ed.D. program is designed to be completed in not more than three years past obtaining the master's, with an expected mean time of completion of two and one-half years after the master's degree. This contrasts sharply with the requirements for the Ph.D. degree, which are to take the equivalent of an academic year in one of the relevant disciplines, a full year of statistics, and a much more theoretical and research-based dissertation. It is anticipated that those students who opt for the Ph.D. degree will recognize that it probably will require a longer period of graduate study, and they will take that option only if they have clearly focused research goals for themselves.

The Core Curriculum

An essential ingredient in the new Program in Administration and Policy Analysis, which is the new title for the concentration, is a first-year core curriculum required for all students regardless of degree levels sought or subconcentration desired. There are powerful arguments against the core curriculum. A major tendency throughout higher education is toward relaxation of requirements rather than toward intensifying them. There is some evidence that many students were attracted to Stanford because its previous program was highly flexible. A prescribed core could conceivably jeopardize application rates. Also, there is the belief that career aspirations are so varied that no core can legitimately serve all matriculants. However, the faculty in administration decided that the reasons favoring a core far outweighed those against it. First, and possibly most significant, because education is complex and becoming ever more so, involving hundreds of specialties, there is increasing need for people at various levels to be able to communicate with each other in sophisticated terms. The school superintendent cannot really function effectively unless he can communicate with the research scholar and utilize results from scholarship. An official working in an educational agency cannot deal adequately with policy questions unless he can communicate with and empathize with the practicing school administrator. Articulation between the lower and higher levels of education is enormously difficult unless administrators at each level know a great deal about the problems of the others. Thus, a core curriculum can be justified on the same ground that general education was justified for undergraduate students: it provides the common universe of discourse needed by all people to function effectively in a complex society. Secondly, as the social and behavioral sciences have matured and as research and scholarship in them has become more focused, these fields can contribute to understanding practice much as the biological sciences came to undergird medical practice in the earlier part of the twentieth century. For most of the period since economics emerged as a specific discipline, economists did not devote attention to educational problems nor was much economic scholarship relevant; the same criticism can be leveled at political science, sociology, psychology, and anthropology. However, during the 1960s work in these fields began to impinge more and more on the practice of education, producing an imperative that practitioners be conversant with them in order to understand and cope with the problems they faced. It now seems reasonable that courses can be developed, based firmly on the social and behavioral sciences, which can speak directly to administrative problems and can serve as keys giving administrators access to the swelling volume of relevant research and scholarship. One of the three year-long courses that will comprise the core in the administration and policy analysis program at Stanford will be an interdisciplinary course drawing largely on economics, political science, and sociology. The decision to emphasize those three disciplines was a difficult one, for it was originally assumed that psychology and anthropology should especially contribute to core understandings. The decision not to include those fields specifically reflected faculty rejection of the concept of comprehensiveness. Unless some limits are imposed, it could be argued that a core should include everything conceivably of value to most practitioners. Such comprehensiveness is patently impossible to achieve. The decision also resulted in part from the perception that psychology as taught in both the School of Education at Stanford and the department of psychology was not oriented to provide insight for future administrators. Interested students could take courses or do readings in psychology and social psychology, and very likely many would do so, but the main emphases in those fields seemed such that a requirement would not be in the best interests of the students. As for anthropology, which could contribute to rectifying an implicit ethnocentrism, it was assumed that many students would elect appropriate courses during the second year and that some elements of comparative education could be included in the core as finally fashioned. For example, a second year-long sequence will deal with the nature of educational institutions in their social context and how they are organized, administered, and governed. Properly structured, that course seemed an ideal vehicle to include some comparative materials—perhaps not as much as might ideally be desired but enough to be effective.

To Create a Sense of Community

The core concept has more than purely curricular argument to support it. Progression through graduate school is frequently an isolated and frustrating experience. Professors have their own research to do and students find themselves, particularly at the dissertation level of study, pursuing a lonely existence. One objective of the new program in administration is to create a sense of community that will interrelate faculty and student interests and can serve as a buttress against individual loneliness. A sense of community can be achieved in many ways, but an important way is through the curriculum. The developments during the 1960s of team teaching, cluster colleges, or houseplans produced important evidence that when students faced common intellectual tasks as a group, morale and esprit de corps increased, as did individual achievement. Even such a simple thing as box-scheduling groups of the same students into three or four courses tended during a single semester to convert those classes into an important primary group. It is expected that the core of three year-long courses taken by an entire cohort group will contribute to this important sense of community. In a free elective system, the odds against two students being in the same three classes are infinitesimal. The prescribed core rectifies that condition. As the core courses produce a cohesive sense of community, that should also facilitate guidance and counseling, ranging from such a simple thing as conveying information on when examinations are to be taken, to complex discussions of career choice. Such matters can be handled in these groups with some assurance that no individuals will be left out. Using the counseling potential of the core courses should make for more efficient use of faculty time.

Decision-Making

The third of the year-long sequences is a course on decision science, which will introduce students to statistics appropriate for decision-making, uses of computers, and tightly organized styles of reasoning. The fundamental reason for such a course is that newer management procedures require that administrators be reasonably sophisticated. But there is also a serendipitous value. The Graduate School of Business, the Department of Communications, and the School of Engineering all offer advanced courses that are highly relevant to future educational administrators, yet most of those advanced courses require a statistical sophistication which previously education students did not possess, nor could they obtain the requisite skills by enrolling in first-year courses in those schools because first-year courses for the most part had strictly limited enrollments. The limitations generally did not extend to second- or third-year courses; thus a new year-long sequence in decision science offered in the School of Education will automatically enrich the potential curriculum through qualifying students to take advanced courses outside the School of Education.

Advanced Courses

Building on the foundation of the first-year core courses are a variety of advanced courses in education with special relevance for administration, advanced courses elsewhere in the School of Education, and courses from elsewhere in the university that can be used either for a minor or to reinforce some particularly desired program pattern. The plan is for these advanced courses to be available for election by students on the advice of the adviser. No specific set of courses are required for any of the three emphases; however, some are logically designed for one of the various subconcentrations. These various courses are advanced in that they build on the core of courses and require reasonably sophisticated synthesis of theory, research, and conceptualization from one or several disciplinary points of view, all brought to bear on problems of educational administration. Some are advanced in the sense that they presuppose some in-depth exposure to the relevant academic discipline in order to cope with the materials of the course. However, they are not advanced in the sense that completion of all of the courses in any one of the sequences—for example, the sequence dealing with economics and finance of education—will produce a specialist. A student who wants to become a specialist in the finance of education, for example, should take not only courses in the School of Education but other specialized courses in economics and in the Graduate School of Business as well.

While all of the advanced courses in the administration and policy analysis program are designed to bear directly on problems and issues faced by practitioners, they do so in varying degrees. Thus there are a cluster of courses deriving from sociology, economics, and political science which are somewhat more theoretically oriented than are other clusters of courses that deal with the actual practices of higher education in elementary and secondary education and in the various agencies, associations, and bureaucracies concerned with educational matters. Obviously, the kinds of courses that can be offered in a graduate school such as Stanford's depend in large measure on the interests and research competencies of individual faculty members. However, the listings of courses have been reviewed by the whole faculty and a serious attempt made to ensure that all major domains or concerns are adequately covered.

The proposed course offerings include the following:

Organizational Change and Innovation
Survey Research, Design, and Analysis
Educational Administration, Decision-Making, and Cultural Pluralism
Planning in Educational Administration
Systems Applications in Education
Schools and Community
Federal Education Policy and Administration
State Education Policy and Administration
The Governance of Elementary Secondary Schools
Workshop in Financing Education
Introduction to Economics of Education
Financial Decision-Making in Education
Seminar in Financing Education
Workshop in Financing Education
Financing Higher Education
Education and Law
Organization of Work and the Training of Manpower
Economics of Education
Leadership in Organizations
Introduction to Models in Social Science
Contemporary Problems in Social Institutions
Advanced Research in Organization Theory
Organizational Decision-Making

Computer Models of Social Behavior
Establishing Higher Educational Policy
Structure and Functioning of Institutions of Higher Education
Technical Problems and Processes in Administration of Higher Education
Literature and Research in Higher Education
Curriculum and Instruction in Higher Education
Education Policy Formulation and Administration
Collective Bargaining
Organizational Learning and Adaptation
Workshop for Dissertation Students in Organization and Policy Analysis
Administration and Organization of Elementary and Secondary Schools
Administration and Organization of Complex Systems of Elementary and Secondary Schools
School Personnel Policies and Practice Analysis
Legal Bases and Implications for Education
Literature and Research in Elementary and Secondary Education
Case and Field Studies in Elementary and Secondary Education

The courses designed for administration and policy analysis are designed in the context of other courses and programs in the School of Education. The Stanford School of Education is not organized by departments but into committees representing areas of concentration. Each committee is comprised of a few faculty members who devote almost full-time to the courses and activities of the area of concentration, and others have multiple assignments. In 1973, in addition to the concentration in administration and policy analysis, there were concentrations in psychological studies, international development, sociohumanistic studies, mathematical and statistical studies, counseling and guidance, curriculum and instruction, and politics and economics of education. In addition, within the School of Education is the Stanford Center for Research and Development in Teaching. Each of these concentrations offers courses and has faculty germane to the needs of graduate students in administrative programs. The selection of such resources is generally the responsibility of individual students and their advisers, with the exception of schoolwide requirements that all students should develop some awareness and competency in several categories of knowledge that cut across the various areas of concentration. All students are expected to be exposed to some strictly professional courses such as administration or curriculum building, something in the social and behavioral sciences, something in the normative domain, some exposure to relevant skills of inquiry and, when appropriate, to a minor field of study.

Generally, it is assumed that considerable use should be made of courses in other areas of concentration. However, several problems arise that can more easily be identified than solved. Within the areas of psychological studies and mathematical and statistical studies, the School of Education possesses great strengths in statistics. However, most of the emphasis is on statistics used in experimentation rather than on the kind of statistical analyses appropriate for decision-making in complex organizations. Thus when the faculty in administration elected to make a full-year sequence stressing quantitative decision-making, prescribing existing courses did not appear to be a good solution. It is hoped, of course, that some of the faculty from those two concentrations can participate in some way in the core course (assuming their other commitments allow it), but the basic responsibility for the core course in decision-making had to be lodged in the committee on administration and policy analysis.

Counseling and Guidance

The concentration in counseling and guidance maintains two emphases: (1) to prepare technically competent school counselors, and (2) to conduct research largely restricted to the behavior modification mode of counseling practice. For a few administration students —for example, those who wish to become deans of students—some work in this concentration is relevant. However, for the more generally oriented administrative candidate, the concentration does not offer a great deal of focus on broader policy considerations on student personnel services, which the future administrator needs to understand. The concentration on international development presents a fertile field for reciprocity, which had already begun and will be cultivated more in the future. Many of the students attracted to that concentration are from foreign countries who very likely will return to their homelands in administrative capacities. Many of the courses in the domain of administration and policy analysis are germane to their interests. Reciprocally, faculty members in international development can offer a significant comparative education point of view to American students. It seems likely that parts of the administrative core will be made available to international students and parts of the international core could become significant electives for administrative students. The direct serviceability of courses in the sociohumanistic domain is much more apparent than real. Courses in history, philosophy, and sociology of education are designed to serve a heterogeneous student body, and they apparently do so. Not much more need be done to assure the contributions of that area to administrative students. However, faculty members in that concentration possess insights that could illuminate materials in the administrative courses themselves. An important future project will be to contrive ways so that faculty members will be willing to assist in some of the administrative courses, notably the core. Probably goodwill will allow this participation for a time. But if the new curriculum in administration is to become firmly institutionalized, formal systems of reciprocity must be worked out.

Evaluation

Curricula for a profession should be constantly evolving, and one of the hopes of the faculty in administration is that over the next several years new configurations can emerge of direct significance for students in many different concentrations. For example, a serious gap in the preparation of administrators is in program and curriculum evaluation. Yet the School of Education faculty possesses great collective strength in evaluation at all levels of education. There is the distinct possibility that individuals from psychological studies, the Center for Research and Development, and from higher education could organize an ad hoc attempt to develop an interdisciplinary and interlevel course or program in evaluation.

Work Outside the School of Education

In the past, the School of Education has made considerable use of courses and faculty outside the school. Candidates for the Ph.D. degree are required to have a minor outside the school of education or a master's degree in an academic subject in lieu of that minor. Candidates for the Ed.D. degree have been required to take at least twelve units outside of the school of education. Compliance with these requirements has been varyingly successful. It has been possible for people to work out minors in political science, sociology, and occasionally history. For several years there has been a joint program between the School of Education and the Graduate School of Business in which students registered first in the Graduate School of Business, and after completion of the M.B.A. degree enrolled in the School of Education for an Ed.D. or Ph.D. program. This was made possible because the allowable electives in the master of business administration could be taken in the School of Education, thus allowing candidates to work off education course requirements while still M.B.A. candidates. Additionally, it has been possible for a few Ph.D. candidates to work out a minor in the Graduate School of Business. However, this has not been completely satisfactory because of the point previously mentioned, that is, only upper-level Graduate School of Business courses were open to education students, who frequently lacked the requisite technical background. There has been continuing cooperation between the School of Education and the School of Law, exemplified by a course on education and law jointly taught by a law professor and a professor of education. Additionally, the two faculties have agreed in principle on a joint law and education program and there is disposition to allow students in each school to work off electives or to take a minor in the other school. In the academic year 1972-73 the first School of Education student was accepted by the Law School as a minor candidate, and although he was required to compete with law school students who had taken many more courses in law, on examinations he was able to meet law school requirements successfully.

Cooperation with Other Schools

One major component of the new program in administration and policy analysis is to intensify the cooperative activities already initiated and to initiate still deeper levels of cooperation. The School of Education and the Law School propose a major effort to obtain external funding for the joint appointment between law and education, in the hopes that such an individual can give direction to a joint law and education program which will be sufficiently successful that it can eventually be assumed by university resources. In addition, it seems likely that one professor in education and one professor in the communications department will be able to develop a survey research course to be jointly taught and of service to both the school and the department. Some of the advanced courses in communications will become available for education students and the core course in administration and policy analysis has elements which the Department of Communications would like to use for its students. Several members of the faculty in the Graduate School of Business teach public policy courses based on case materials that are of direct relevance to education students. These will be opened to education students, but in addition there is a willingness (subject to appropriate exchange of financing) for reciprocal exchange of faculty which will enable each school to rectify some deficiencies. Given time and some additional financial resources, this sort of cooperation will be extended to other schools and departments. One can be rather sanguine that this can happen, partly because of the large number of joint or courtesy appointments already in existence and partly by the generally favorable attitude toward School of Education faculty and students on the part of other units of the university. In some institutions, schools of education function somewhat in isolation. That situation is much less aggravated at Stanford.

Participation by Outside Faculty

An institution as complex as Stanford University has many individuals serving in administrative and management capacities whose knowledge and insights are directly relevant to students of administration. In the past, several administrators have held courtesy appointments in the School of Education. The intent now is, not necessarily to offer courtesy appointments, but to invite individuals from the various administrative units of the institution to participate in the program in varying ways. The president, for example, has indicated a willingness to appear periodically in seminars dealing with the administration of higher education. Similarly, the vice-president for finance and various officers in the Office of the Provost have also expressed willingness to serve, and indeed have participated in the past by serving on appropriate dissertation committees. Other individuals, provided they can arrange their time, have expressed willingness to offer a full course. The willingness of central administration to participate is indicated by the fact that administrative offices at Stanford have accepted for the academic year 1973-74 the largest number ever of paid interns, and have indicated a desire to institutionalize that kind of activity. The faculty for administration and policy analysis plans to expand use of Stanford faculty and administration in order to provide a richness and variety of program a small faculty is incapable of mounting by itself.

The Need for Field Experience

Students and former students all testify to the need for some internship or field experience activity as an essential of an academic program in administration. For almost twenty years the School of Education maintained a School Planning Laboratory, which graduated some sixty individuals. When queried, they universally claimed that the field experiences growing out of the laboratory work were the most valuable part of their Stanford experience. Yet the faculty in administration and policy analysis was until recently unable to mount a satisfactory internship or field part of the program. Most individuals who wanted an applied component could be at least partially satisfied through various ad hoc arrangements. However, these were far from satisfactory, for students could not plan on an internship at a definite point in their career, nor could the problem of supervision be easily solved, given other commitments of faculty members. Additionally, no faculty time was allocated to conduct a seminar or colloquium to accompany fieldwork, partly because of lack of faculty and partly because there was no consistent pattern of when internship or fieldwork activities would be undertaken. Experience elsewhere has raised a number of questions as to the values of internships. They do frequently degenerate into students doing routine tasks. They do suffer from lack of consistent supervision. And, adequately done, they are expensive. In spite of those objections, the faculty has adopted as a requirement for the Ed.D. degree a definite internship period to be accompanied by a seminar or colloquium that will relate field experience to academic insight. Occasionally, an individual may have had such relevant work experience that the internship can be waived. But it is expected that those instances will be rare indeed. It is also anticipated that some Ph.D. candidates would profit from an internship and provisions are also being made to include those persons in the sustained program to be developed.

Internships

The full internship program is expected to begin in fall 1974. However, a modified program was launched for the academic year 1973, and its essential characteristics will prevail in the new program. There should be a variety of types of internships in which both the educational needs of students and the needs of host institutions are merged. There should not be an elimination of routine work but rather a judicious blending of routine and more creative activities. Host institutions may choose to lodge an intern in only one office or may allow him to move into several different offices. Whichever pattern is followed, the intern is expected to view one activity in depth and to sample reasonably widely other sorts of activities. While the duration of internships can vary to some extent, the optimum would be a half-time commitment for each of two quarters in the second year of a doctoral program. This would be associated with a parallel seminar or colloquium which would bring interns serving in quite different conditions together to relate theory to practice and to exchange ideas and experiences. To assign proper value to the internship as well as to help students financially, remuneration is judged essential. Thus a major responsibility in adhering to the program in administration and policy analysis is to ensure that interns prove to be sufficiently valuable to warrant continued financial support by the host institution.

Services to the Community

University service to the field and university relationships with the surrounding community are closely linked with internships and field experiences. The litany for American universities prescribes three principal functions: teaching, research, and service. The archetype is the land grant university, with its agricultural extension service, university extension service, and a relatively rich program of short courses, summer conferences and workshops, and the like. A school of education in a land grant university has an existing structure and a method for financing extensive programs of service. In addition to on-campus teaching and research, such schools conduct statewide testing programs, provide consultative services to school districts, conduct courses for credit in school plants, convene statewide conferences on such matters as articulation or the uses of computer-based instruction, operate full summer school programs designed specifically to upgrade educational workers, and mount many different summer workshops to facilitate educational renewal. While nominal fees may be charged clients for some of these activities, the basic financial support is provided through specific state appropriations and is regarded as a legitimate expense chargeable to taxpayers. Similarly, publicly supported institutions are expected to maintain close liaison with their surrounding communities and to differentiate their programs according to differing community needs.

Privately supported universities confront a different situation. As universities, they are expected to fulfill a service obligation; however, their revenues are frequently designated for different purposes by different constituencies. Thus, students pay tuition as a fee for educational services rendered. Research grants and contracts obviously require performance of specific actions. Unrestricted endowment is expected to be used first for the maintenance of the campus and its educational programs and for generally accepted research activities of the faculty. Only if teaching and research were completely supported would there be justification for expending funds for extension work or continuing education. An option, of course, is for the private university to offer services for which it is qualified and to charge fees sufficient to underwrite the entire activity. This, however, raises the spectre of competition, which the private institution can meet only if there is demonstrable, qualitative difference. For example, in the early 1960s Stanford, UCLA, and the University of California at Berkeley all conducted summer workshops for junior college administrators. Individuals could participate in a three-week workshop at Berkeley for a fee of $60, or attend Stanford for the same length of time but for a fee of $200, with comparable room and board rates. The economic advantage clearly lay with the public institutions. The fact that Stanford was able to recruit larger numbers of participants than did the public institutions could perhaps be attributed to the greater tranquillity of the Stanford campus, possibly to some program differences, and probably to some latent alumni loyalty. As the price gap widens between the public and private institutions, as it did during the late 1960s and the early 1970s, the appeal of such qualitative differences weakens.

The Question of Field Service

There are persuasive reasons why a school of education like Stanford's should engage in field service. The faculty has expertise that could help schools, school systems, and colleges and universities solve some of their problems. Service activities—for example, consulting or conducting surveys—can provide valuable clinical experience for students in training. If the funding problem were solved, many service activities provide a natural way to support graduate students financially. The field is fertile ground for conducting educational research and for field-testing practices and techniques developed under tightly controlled experimental conditions; a functioning array of services facilitates entry into that research terrain. In addition, if a school of education is constantly available to offer a range of services, that fact alone can facilitate placement of graduates and could conceivably help generate gift income.

On the other hand, there are cogent reasons why the faculty in administration and policy analysis at Stanford should *not* embark on an elaborate field services undertaking. The faculty is small and carries a heavy load of teaching, advising, and research. The time spent in service activities simply means that other critical duties must be de-emphasized. A minor, but nonetheless significant, side issue is the matter of remuneration. Most of the faculty members are in heavy demand as consultants or field survey directors, for which they are given extra remuneration—made possible through the university's policy of encouraging one day a week spent in remunerated consulting activity. Providing service through institutional auspices thus restricts the extra compensation available to faculty members. Then, too, many of the faculty are engaged primarily in research that is several steps removed from the ongoing problems of school or college administration. Direct service thus can detract from the energy and motivation directed toward more basic research activities.

Stanford's resolution of the issue as to whether or not to emphasize field services involved a compromise. The faculty was in general agreement about the values of field services, and agreed that each faculty member should, insofar as his own interests and time allowed, extend the range of service that he and his students should draw not only on administration faculty but faculty from other concentrations as well, so that if a special unit were to be organized it should be at the school rather than at the concentration level. The recommendation was that the School of Education investigate whether or not it could create a field services unit, and support it primarily through fees charged. Given other imperatives requiring university support there was no disposition to suggest that field services with university underwriting should occupy a position of high priority. This decision illustrated once again the faculty's belief that program comprehensiveness was an unobtainable goal. The primary mission of the faculty in administration and policy analysis is to provide an intellectually demanding curriculum for a limited number of students who wish to hold high administrative positions. Their education should contain relevant field experiences, but as long as these can be contrived under less structured conditions, field services do not appear to be likely for the immediate future.

A more active posture seemed desirable for various summer-in-service training programs and for limited continuing education programs such as acceptance of postdoctoral students for residency at Stanford. The faculty generally agreed that through the 1970s and the early 1980s the turnover of incumbents in administrative positions would probably be considerably less than in the past. Yet new techniques and knowledge of significance to administrators continue to increase almost exponentially. Since the faculty for administration and policy analysis is constantly dealing with this increase in knowledge, it seemed reasonable that it could mount summer programs, with each faculty member agreeing to summer school work approximately once every three years. It was also agreed that a limited number of practitioners could be invited each year as postdoctoral students or as visiting scholars. Such individuals, using, for example, sabbatical leaves from their own institutions, could be absorbed into the Stanford community without placing a serious time or financial demand on the faculty; they could also contribute insights from the field to the community of mature and maturing scholars in the Stanford program.

Admissions

Assuming a relatively small student body along with a fairly large applicant pool, the question then arose as to the criteria for admissions. At earlier times admission to the Stanford curricula in administration required prior educational experience, in part contingent on state credentialing requirements. However, as state credential requirements have been modified the rationale for an experience requirement has lost some of its force. Even without the requirement, past admissions were based on faculty judgments made on the basis of a student's statement of purpose, previous academic record, scores on the graduate record examination, previous work experience, and letters of recommendation. There is some uneasiness that judgments made in this way are unreliable, unrelated to subsequent academic performance, and indeed at times almost capricious. Several alternatives seemed possible. The first would be to seek greater reliability through having all faculty members judge on contrived scales the full range of information. This has several virtues: it involves all faculty in the admissions process and it allows some weight to subjective impressions. However, logistically it is difficult to operate and is extraordinarily demanding of faculty time. To handle existing rates of application would require each faculty member to devote some sixty hours to reading and evaluating applications, and this does not count the time spent on reconciling differences in judgment. However, asking a single faculty member or a small group to use the same subjective criteria would tend to reduce reliability.

A second option theoretically has much to recommend it, but is unrealistic from the standpoint of either political relationships or public image. This alternative would require some technique for deciding quickly which applicants are clearly inadmissible, and would then use the lottery system for selecting from the admissible pool.

The third alternative would be much more mechanistic, combining previous academic record and measured academic aptitude and then selecting those with the highest numerical rankings. Such a system runs counter to a growing belief that grades and aptitude are not positively related to subsequent professional performance. It also seemingly jeopardizes applicants from minority groups who have not performed well on tests or other forms of measurement of academic achievement. However, achievement and aptitude are positively related to the kinds of activities carried on in a graduate school, and apparently there are no other predictors of subsequent professional achievement that are usable. Given the ethos of American democracy, it would be possible, for example, to predict levels of professional attainment through a formula that would include race, mother's education, father's occupation, father's income, and average family income for the preceding three generations. Such an equation would be patently unacceptable.

Again, compromise resulted in policy. Basically, admissions will be

based on a combination of academic achievement and academic aptitude. Particularly relevant work experience may be assigned some
weight, as will clarity of professional purpose. Applicants coming
from groups against which formal testing operates are to be considered in a separate pool, but still examined to determine academic aptitude. Very likely interviews and telephone questioning of infor-
mants will be used widely.

How Many Degrees?

American academic degree structure has historically been chaotic
and has resulted in the excessively large number of discrete degrees,
somewhere between 1,600 and 2,000. The fact that only an approx-
imation can be given is indicative of the chaos. As the faculty in administration and policy analysis pondered its degree needs, it tried to
apply the principles of an ideal degree structure developed by
Spurr.[1] Spurr urges that:

(1) The number of different degree titles should be kept as low as
possible.

(2) Degree structure should be flexible in terms of the time required for completion of the academic program, to encourage accel-
eration, but should have specific overall time limits to discourage too
attenuated an effort.

(3) Each degree should mark the successful completion of one
stage of academic progress without implications or prejudgment as to
a student's capacity to embark on following stages.

(4) Degree structures should be so interrelated that the maximum
opportunity exists for redirection as the student's motivation, interests, and intellectual achievements permit.

(5) The various components of the educational experience should
not be optimally separable into different time periods. The degree
structure in administration and policy analysis consists of three degrees: the master's, the Ed.D., and the Ph.D. Both the Ed.D. and the
Ph.D. are so organized that they can conceivably be completed in as
few as two years after receiving the master's, but the desired upper
limit is three years for the Ed.D. and four to five years for the Ph.D.
The master's degree is conceived of as a degree for one year of full-
time work; however, the program could be enriched through one or
two summer sessions. The master's is viewed as a discrete entity signi-
fying successful completion of a well-conceived educational program.

It is to be awarded to all students who complete successfully the first full year in the graduate program in administration and policy analysis, regardless of whether the candidate had matriculated for a master's program only or for a doctoral program.

Ideally, to be consistent with Spurr's theory, no students would be admitted for anything other than a master's program; at the end of the first year the decision is made as to which students will and which will not continue their graduate work. The drawback is that such a policy might not be sufficiently competitive, for many students with clear vocational goals want the satisfaction of matriculating for the final degree to which they aspire. The heavy prescribed course load during the first year is intended to facilitate flexibility. This core is required of all students and therefore becomes a common legal tender which can be extended for a research program, a practitioner program culminating in the Ed.D., or a practitioner program culminating in the master's degree. It is expected that the counseling and guidance capabilities which the core program allows will facilitate changes in student's career plans during the first year. Such an arrangement is adopted at the cost of Spurr's fifth principle, which argues that the various components of a curriculum should be spread over a three- or four-year period. The core requirement implies that internships or field experiences are taken during the second year and that research assistantships are granted during the third year of formal study. However, through such extracurricular devices as the student-operated colloquium, it is hoped that some of the applied component of the program can be injected into the first year, thus approximating the spread of experiences over each of the years the students are involved in the program.

Conclusion

We have outlined the rationales that underlie the new curriculum in administration and policy analysis in the School of Education at Stanford. The ways in which these are to be implemented are indicated in the guidelines in the appendix.

Note

1. Stephen H. Spurr, *Academic Degree Structures: Innovative Approaches* (New York: McGraw-Hill, 1970), pp. 26-28.

4. Processes of
Curriculum Building

Approaches to Curriculum Building

In theory, constructing a curriculum should be a straightforward and rational process. This supposition stands forth clearly when one examines some of the major theoretical attempts to systematize curriculum construction. In the 1920s W. W. Charters, seeking to modernize Stephens College in Columbia, Missouri, developed an approach to task analysis that he believed could produce a rational and effective curriculum. Charters asked several hundred college-educated women to keep detailed diaries for several weeks in which they recorded their various activities. Each activity became an item of behavior to be classified and reclassified, until a taxonomy of nine areas of behavior was produced. Then, in what Charters called "educational engineering," he led the faculty to construct courses designed to develop the specific behaviors implicit in the nine categories, and the nine categories eventually became the nine principal academic units of the institution.

This exercise produced several significant curricular modifications for that particular time in history. Sex, marriage, and the family proved, not surprisingly, to be the major components of women's lives, and the college developed a few of the first courses dealing with those matters anywhere in the country. Managing the family budget also figured large, and as a result early prototype courses on consumer spending were developed.

A decade later, and quite probably as a result of some of the same factors that influenced Charters, Ralph W. Tyler developed an approach to curriculum building almost elegant in its symmetry and rationality. First, Tyler contended, the educator should posit broad desirable objectives that are essentially value statements for such goals as effective citizenship, critical thinking, or aesthetic appreciation. These are then converted into statements of the specific behaviors manifested by people judged to have achieved or to possess the qualities implied by the broad objectives. Once these statements have been made and listed in some hierarchical order of importance, the educator should find appropriate learning activities deemed likely to produce the kinds of behaviors specified. Assuming that quest is successful, the next step is to develop instruments or devices to test whether or not individuals have indeed developed the desired behaviors. Once such information is available, it can be related back to the original statements of broad objectives and judgments made as to the success or failure, appropriateness or inappropriateness, adequacy or inadequacy, of the entire process.

Tyler's basic ideas have been refined in a number of ways and have been used with limited success in some curriculum building. Benjamin S. Bloom and his associates collected hundreds of educationally significant specific behavioral objectives and ordered them into a three-domain taxonomy: cognitive, affective, and psychomotor. Some programs in general education were developed, using at least in part Tyler's system of analysis. In a few professional fields, e.g., nursing and engineering, and eventually, in a few institutions, architecture and medicine, Tyler's approach was also attempted. Most of the curricular theorists who have written since Tyler have developed some variant on his rational mode of analysis. Dressel translated specific behaviors into specific competencies toward the achievement of which curricula should be organized. Phenix clustered specific objectives into several broad categories, which he called "realms of meaning." Mayhew and Ford attempted an eclectic approach listing desired behaviors as competencies and effective learning experiences as desired experiences. They achieved some degree of symmetry through using clusters somewhat akin to the realms of meaning of Phenix or the earlier family of behaviors used by Charters.

Barriers to a Rational Curriculum

Yet college curricula rarely reveal such rationality and faculties rarely put themselves through the laborious efforts needed to develop curricula in so logical a way. Several reasons can be suggested to explain why this is so. Perhaps the primary reason is the proprietary right that faculty members feel toward the courses they teach, which are based on their own interests. Faculty members in their graduate training become specialists in limited fields, and they publish the results of their specialized study in books, articles, and monographs, or, more frequently, in the form of specialized courses. Since their own interests govern their specialized fields of study it would be quite accidental if those interests conformed to some broad curricular pattern. This conflict is clearly revealed in the general education movement which gained strength in the late 1940s and 1950s. General education courses were those courses presumed desirable for all students to prepare them for their nonvocational lives as citizens, family members, and self-actualizing persons. The courses were composite ones developed by faculties and taught by faculty members, regardless of their own field of specialization. Thus historians, philosophers, musicologists, and specialists in literature would all teach the same course in the humanities. As long as qualified professors were in oversupply institutions could require that faculty members teach these staff courses. However, by the end of the 1950s the faculty supply situation had changed markedly and faculty members were able to resist requirements to teach staff courses, naturally preferring to teach those things they had studied intensively as graduate students. There were, of course, other factors operating, but this staff factor seems to be the most significant in accounting for the demise of general education as a major educational tendency. As indicated in chapter 3, the curriculum in the School of Education at Stanford reflected this proprietary posture; in administration, for example, the curriculum consisted of courses of specific interest to individual faculty members, with some slight obeisance to courses required for state credentialing purposes. Even those strictures, however, were so loosely applied that the real task for a faculty member developing a course was to organize what he wanted to teach in such a way that it apparently met specifications of the state education code.

A second barrier to a rational curriculum is the general lack of awareness among faculties about what behaviors individuals will really need to perform roles for which undergraduate or graduate education has been judged appropriate preparation. The task of systematically surveying behaviors of those in the field frequently transcends the time or resources that a faculty can use for such inquiries, and data, even if gathered, is often seen as suspect if it doesn't conform to the specialized anticipations of a professor who functions in an academic setting. Faculties in professional schools, particularly in more academically prestigious institutions, have quite casual and specialized contacts with practitioners in the field and as a result have accumulated only rudimentary beliefs about what talents should be encouraged and what traits developed in their students. Sounding almost like caricatures are such examples as a professor modifying a course because of letters received from particularly satisfied, or dissatisfied, alumni, or professors who say they know alumni want specifically detailed training in this or that skill but such training is really not the responsibility of the theoretically or research oriented university.

But even if a professional faculty systematically accumulated information on needed traits or talents, there is considerable uncertainty as to how pedagogically to develop them. Schools of business and law have concentrated on cases as desirable and appropriate teaching techniques, and medicine has exposed its students to daily observation of patients, but when one examines the range of presumed professional needs and the range of instructional techniques utilized, one is struck by the magnitude of illogicality or misfit between the two. Thus schools of architecture stress urban design through lectures and fieldwork on the urban condition, schools of engineering approach design problems through lectures, discussions, and laboratories in physics, chemistry, and mathematics, and schools of education approach principles of administration through textbook readings, lectures, discussions, and some casual observation. This condition, if the description is faithful to reality, gives point to the term offered by James G. March of Stanford University: "organized anarchy." The university is unsure of its goals, even less sure of the efficacy of the technology to achieve those goals, and virtually without means of assessing successes or failures.

Developing a reasonably logical and rich curriculum in schools of education (or for that matter, other professional schools) is made more difficult by barriers between schools and other units of a university, even when a case could be made for cooperation. Presumably many courses in arts and sciences, as well as in schools of business or law, might be relevant to a balanced training program for educational administrators. Yet barriers between schools make student access to outside courses difficult, and because those courses were designed with other purposes in mind, the clear relevance for educational administration is too frequently obscured. As was mentioned earlier, one of the major tasks which the faculty in administration at Stanford undertook was to achieve ways of opening up resources outside the School of Education that could be of significance in producing a balanced program. Opening up those courses is, however, only the first step. A more difficult one is, for example, to convince a professor of business to include educational materials in a course in public policy. In a sense the very request that he do so jeopardizes his own professional interests and concerns.

Very real ideological differences do exist which can split or polarize faculties, making a staff-developed curriculum difficult if not impossible to achieve. Some faculty members are oriented toward research and see as their principal obligation reproducing themselves in the young research workers they train. Others who have had more applied experience oppose this, with the issues frequently being joined on such questions as approval or disapproval of dissertation topics, or sending or not sending students into each other's courses. Contemporarily there is a split over quantification. Some believe that most social phenomena can be best understood through reducing them to numbers and then manipulating the resultant statistics. Others feel that a preoccupation with quantification is excessively narrow and misses the variety and intensity that characterize real-life situations. Such differences as these clearly existed within the faculty for administration at Stanford and the major challenge was to discover whether those differences could be harmonized to produce a better training program, or whether they were so entrenched as to preclude genuinely cooperative education.

Related is the matter of personal animosity, which is present in all organizations and must be minimized if it is not to act as a substantial barrier to rational curricular development. Frequently personal animosity derives from basic ideological differences; e.g., the advocate of behavioral modification feels that his system is so reflective of reality that he comes to question the judgment or even the integrity of a Freudian-oriented scientist. In recent years entire professional schools have been virtually paralyzed through the schisms produced by such animosities. One Midwestern school of social work reached the point at which behavior modification advocates ceased speaking with those of other persuasions. It required the appointment of a new dean and the resignation of several of the most intransigent faculty members before tranquillity could be restored.

A major barrier to systematic curriculum building is simply the lack of time disposable for planning purposes in the face of other professional obligations or activities of faculty members. Especially in a research-oriented university, faculty members must meet classes, counsel graduate students, conduct their own research, seek external support for anticipated research, consult, participate in regional or national policy activities, and attend to a modicum of necessary departmental or institutional administrative duties. Planning a consistent curriculum requires a great deal of face-to-face discussion, which inevitably involves considering matters that some judge to be irrelevant or of no consequence, and these meetings must be sustained over time. The time is all too frequently not available, as exemplified by a recent attempt at Stanford to find a free hour twice a week when an eight-member committee could meet to consider improvement of instruction; when all members cancelled out those times their own priorities made unavailable, only one hour remained as a possibility, and presumably that would be cut into by other demands for a few faculty members.

Another barrier to curriculum planning and course development is the standard budget process now in operation in most collegiate institutions. The larger portion of the instructional budget goes for faculty salaries and is justified through course contact hours. Budgets rarely provide for substantial planning time, and even more rarely make provisions to develop instructional materials and to experiment with instructional or curricular technology. The rational Tyler approach to curriculum building implies a rather intensive search for learning materials, but budgets typically do not support faculty activity of that sort, nor has a research-oriented faculty been interested in extending such efforts.

A last major barrier, already implied above, is a lack of a technology or the time to use the technology to obtain evaluative evidence as to how programs actually perform. Testing is generally linked to courses and is idiosyncratic to the beliefs of faculty members. Formal evaluations such as qualifying or oral examinations are for the most part demonstrably unreliable, there being little evidence as to how performance in those situations relates to subsequent professional performance. Attempts to evaluate graduates too frequently become accumulations of opinions on how various parts of their education affect their conduct as professionals. Occasionally a professional school will mount a major evaluation effort that proves to be extraordinarily costly and produces evidence that has little utility for the faculty. For example, in 1968 the Department of Administration at Western Washington State College developed an elaborate program for the supervision of student teachers, some of whom followed traditional modes while others gained their experience under the supervision of practicing teachers in uniquely contrived school settings. Evaluation was done by panels of observers paid to observe former practice teachers in the first and second years after entry into actual teaching. The whole effort generated an enormous amount of information, of such magnitude and complexity that faculty members could not comprehend its significance unless they had played an essential part in the research design. In the absence of persuasive evidence about which parts of a program do or do not function, faculty members can feel quite justified in proceeding in their own idiosyncratic ways.

Devices for Curriculum Change

In spite of the barriers, the essential rationality of professional life and professional schools requires that at least periodic searches be undertaken for new and hopefully more effective ways to reform the curriculum. These generally take one of several principal forms.

By far the most frequently employed device for curriculum change and development is simple accretion based on changing faculty interests, changing faculty members, or changes in credentialing or in the requirements of various boards. A faculty member may shift his interest from collegiate curriculum to academic governance, and the professional curriculum changes accordingly. A new faculty member is appointed and wants to offer those courses that most reflect his present interests—the curriculum in administration is a clear example of this kind of curriculum construction. At Stanford, a professor interested in the history of higher education gave the program one emphasis, which was changed when he retired and was replaced by a professor more interested in contemporary issues. School finance as taught by a professor with experience in the finance office of a state department of education changed radically when that individual became dean and was replaced by an economist who had more theoretical interests.

This approach is not completely bad as long as there is an overarching curricular theory to guide staffing policy. But when curricular needs give way to other considerations, such as a criterion for staffing, serious educational imbalances are likely to appear. In the School of Education at Stanford, staffing policy in the late 1960s made at least the administration faculty dysfunctional with respect to the expectations of graduate students. Faculty members were appointed not because of particularly relevant applied experience, but because of the quality and prestige of their research potential. Their new courses obviously reflected their interests, but students continued to apply to Stanford in hopes of gaining definite and salable skills needed in the administrative work market.

A second major approach to curriculum change lies in conducting institutional self-studies, which generally culminate in long series of recommendations. Self-studies are generally of two sorts. The first is the periodic requirement of some accrediting body for a self-study that is not connected with a review for accreditation. For the most part studies so conducted have not been particularly productive of change or reform; in part because they are defensive instruments they are intended to show the school or the institution in the best light to those legitimately entitled to make judgments. The second sort is the self-study generated by a school or institution in the awareness that abuses have crept in and that some changes are in order. These may be financed by the institution itself or through external funding. During the 1950s, for example, over a score of remarkable institutional self-studies were completed, sponsored by the Ford Foundation. The one conducted at Stanford, published under the title "The Undergraduate and the University," has been judged in part responsible for the significant changes in Stanford University that took place during the 1960s. The source or the origin of a particular self-study may be a chief administrative officer, student pressure or demands, or even occasionally faculty dissatisfaction. However, self-studies typically are conducted in similar ways. Some steering committee sets the broad parameters of the study and assigns subunits, either ad hoc or already existing committees or departments, to investigate various elements of the program. Recommendations are made, collated, and eventually produced in a report, and the recommendations then move through normal decision-making channels for implementation. Unfortunately the form of the massive institutional self-study has not proved to be particularly effective in accomplishing educational change. Ladd, after examining eleven major institutional self-studies, generalizes that "unhappily the results of these studies seem to lend support—at least in a negative way —to the efficacy of pressure politics as a way of bringing about change. There is little indication in any of the experiences to support the idea that the study and report technique is an effective way of gaining acceptance of the need for change, or of creating enthusiasm for involvement in developing new policies. Where the study and report processes were intended primarily to challenge the status quo they largely failed to do so. When the essential objective was to develop the details of a change in the status quo after the community had already accepted the need for some change the study and report processes were much more effective."[1] He goes on to remark that the situations he reviewed "suggest that these studies have rarely succeeded in bringing about any fundamental change in educational policies on the campuses involved, except where a significant portion of the faculty had accepted the desirability of some change before the study began, or where pressures for change from outside the faculties were much in evidence."[2] Because Ladd's insights into the processes of institutional self-study are so penetrating, his analysis is summarized below.[3]

> Committees responsible for institutional self-studies generally proved to be effective and dedicated working groups. In spite of heavy research and consulting commitments, these faculty members were willing to devote long hours to the frustrating matter of discussing educational

policy and reform. Members of the committee testified that they quickly learned to work together, although the ability to work with others was not used as a criterion in selecting committee membership. This ability to work together did produce considerable consensus within the committee even though membership frequently originally contained people of widely differing points of view. In general, institutional research committee members felt a genuine sense of satisfaction when they completed their tasks and the results were generally applauded by most other constituencies on the campus.

However, the fact that study committees worked effectively as committees did not particularly increase their impact on the institution of which they were a part. They were for the most part unable to overcome the absence of institution-wide acceptance of the need for change, nor were they able to compensate for lack of effective leadership which could contrive final implementation. The committees seemed sensitive to the need to ensure wide participation by all constituencies on the campus and they used such devices as open hearings and inviting written and oral submissions to generate the needed input. Even after such diligent efforts, however, widespread awareness of the study did not ensure successful results. This probably is attributable to the propensity of many individuals not to face up to issues until absolutely necessary, and the tendency of many to avoid early commitment to possible change that might affect them and their work. This is not to imply that some other technique such as the sudden presentation of a study report would have been any more effective. It seems just the nature of academic and bureaucratic man to resist innovation and change.

Each of the self-study reports which Ladd examined appeared to be based on some fundamental views about higher education and about the particular institution being considered. Recommendations seem to be related to such common understandings. However, the studies do not reflect any serious debate over fundamental and educational philosophy, nor do they reflect any detailed consideration of the implications of a particular set of recommendations. For example, the reports generally recommend a decrease in the requirements imposed upon students. However, they did not go into the details of making operational a program of counseling and guidance which would seem to be imperative if requirements are diminished. An overall criticism of the studies is that they proposed rather fundamental changes without analyzing the underlying changes in philosophy implied by the recommendations.

All the studies present pertinent evidence that skillful leadership is mandatory for the success of any serious effort at educational reform. Faculty members tend to be quite independent and fiercely jealous of their departments and departmental powers and prerogatives. Given that milieu, the primary task of academic leadership is to try to counter pressures favoring the status quo by creating or maintaining an atmosphere of receptivity to change. However, what the institutional self-studies examined also indicate is that the initiation of major studies alone is not a particularly good technique. What is needed is the willingness and the skill to work with the collegial process of decision-making so that ideas can be moved logically from one decision-making group to another. Thus the effective educational leader must have a keen sense of timing and priorities and an ability to keep things moving in an orderly fashion without appearing to force issues. Such abilities unfortunately were not greatly in evidence in many of the self-studies. Momentum was frequently lost, groups were allowed to take up the wrong things at the wrong time, and discussions were permitted to become contentious and irritating. It should be pointed out that this desired leadership, when exercised, does not necessarily come from the top. At one institution a president would lead, but at several others deans exercised the initiative and at one a professor assumed that role. The lack of manifestation of effective leadership does not imply that colleges and universities possess less than their share of leadership ability. Rather, it seems to derive from the very nature of the collegial structure, which through requiring consensus of any

conflicting groups almost inevitably slows down the decision-making process.

One factor that may very well be involved is institutional size. Among the institutions studied by Ladd, the one in
which the most profound changes were actually made was
the smaller and had the most homogenous of constituencies. In the larger heterogenous institutions change appeared difficult, if not impossible, to bring about. This observation leads to the bleak question as to whether United
States educational policy is essentially incompatible with
reform. Large institutions have become the rule, but large
institutions are almost impossible to change. One can won-
der whether or not the trend toward monolithic institutions has not hit the point of diminishing returns.

A third generally attempted device is some form of a centralized
curriculum committee which reviews and acts on requests for curricular change or suggests promising lines of curricular development.
Such committees have been particularly in vogue in limited-purpose
liberal arts colleges and have frequently been judged to have exerted
a creative influence over curriculum development. When the curriculum committee concept has been employed in more complex institutions it generally ends up either giving pro forma approval to all requests or spending endless hours raising questions of specific detail
that must then be worked out through political processes. A few professional schools have used the curriculum committee, which generally seems to have given most attention to any required courses
deemed desirable and relatively perfunctory review of other courses
suggested by individual faculty members. The curriculum committee
does not seem to have been particularly generative of new patterns of
courses, nor to have contrived greater consistency among the various
concentrations in the school program.

A fourth technique for effecting curricular change is much less frequently used although it has been employed with some degree of success at a few institutions: this is some agency which deliberately sets
about producing small-scale innovations in hope that these will infil-
trate other portions of the school or institution. Perhaps the best
example was the Center for Research in Education at MIT, created
by Professor Jerrold R. Zacharias and funded largely with external
financial support. It attempted many things, such as freeing some

students from the excessive requirements at MIT and developing new forms of individualized learning. In a sense the center placed itself in competition with existing courses in physics or engineering. However, student opinion was so strongly supportive of the freer sorts of curricula that other areas in the university began to change and an overall reduction in the number of required courses was brought about. For such a center to operate effectively the leadership probably must possess an impeccable scholarly reputation as well as considerable political power. For an academician less than highly regarded to attempt to use such a technique seems almost certain to invite disaster, and to relegate students who select the options to second-class academic citizenship. The innovative center seems to have worked well at Stanford through the creation of a series of courses in international relations of such high quality as to illustrate how some departments might modify their courses to resemble the specially contrived courses offered by the Committee on International Relations Education. The MIT Center seems to have been effective because of the internal power and national visibility of Professor Zacharias; he could offer a competing course in physics that would be acceptable to the university and to the departments requiring physics as a prerequisite for more specialized work. It is doubtful if a junior or less prestigious faculty member could have made the center work.

The Process for Curriculum Change Used at Stanford

The process used by the faculty in administration of the School of Education at Stanford to study and modify its curriculum made use of elements of other approaches to curriculum change. In the 1950s Stanford conducted an intensive self-study and an intensive long-range planning effort, which served as background for a decision to try to move Stanford University into the first ranks of American universities, stressing academic excellence, graduate work, and research. Almost from its founding the institution had been a strong regional university, serving bright, but frequently underachieving, children of California upper-middle and upper classes. Its early recognition beyond the West Coast was associated with its strong professional schools of law, business, engineering, and education on the Palo Alto campus, and medicine in San Francisco. During the 1960s Stanford became more selective in admitting undergraduates, improved its departments in humanities and science, and continued to strengthen its professional schools. Toward the end of the decade, however, the university decided that more self-study was in order if the institution was to accommodate the rapid changes brought forth during the late 1960s, and adapt to what increasingly were seen as potentially profound changes during the 1970s and 1980s. The university organized itself through an interacting hierarchy of committees and subcommittees to conduct a study of education at Stanford, which became a ten-volume institutional self-study containing literally hundreds of recommendations ranging from reducing requirements for the undergraduate curriculum to changing the locus for counseling and guidance services. No sooner was the basic work on that study completed and its fiscal implications comprehended than the university began to run into a serious financial situation, in which expenditures were increasing at a much faster rate than was income. Experienced and anticipated deficit spending made imperative the long-range fiscal study, which of course could not be made without careful examination of program and staffing developments. Through a four-year budget adjustment program the university attempted to bring rates of expenditure and income into balance and to establish a base so that the institution could function in a steady state during the 1970s and 1980s. At the same time the university launched a $300,000,000 fund campaign, which if successful, and coupled with the budget adjustments on both sides of the ledger sheet, should place the institution in a viable situation. During this time the various schools and departments of the university, to varying degrees, undertook studies of themselves and their futures. The School of Education was one of the units that began a serious inquiry into its own future under the leadership of a new dean, Arthur P. Coladarci. The Committee on the Futures was appointed, its members freed from teaching for a full term, and it solicited judgments from faculty, students, and alumni and formulated some broad goals along with a recommendation that a number of task forces be appointed, each to deliberate on problems in specific areas of concentration and to recommend for the future. The task forces operating in several different styles made their reports, which were submitted together with responses from the committees representing the major areas of concentration. All this was discussed at great length by the Committee on Academic Affairs, usually in the presence of the dean. After receiving all input Dean

Coladarci developed a broadly constructed set of priorities and guidelines for the future and then asked the faculty for its approval in
principle and for a ranking of priorities. While the resultant chart of
direction was not radically different from the traditional evolution of
the School of Education, it did make explicit several principles and
indicated several new directions. The specific recommendations most
relevant to the work of the Committee on Administration and Policy
Analysis are indicated below:

> *Recommendation:* That a program in Educational Ad-
> ministration, Finance, and Organization be continued with
> the request that it include opportunities to prepare, at
> M.A. and doctoral levels, for administrative roles.
>
> *Recommendation:* That a search committee be formed
> immediately to find a faculty member for 1973-74 in the
> area of educational administration with experience and
> training appropriate to the preparation for administrative
> roles and research in this domain.

While these developments were taking place the faculty in administration was experiencing a number of frustrations and perplexities. It
seemed to be serving an extraordinarily large number of students—a
number exceeding its capabilities—but had no generally acceptable
way of reducing that number. The department members were generally aware that its curriculum was dysfunctional with the needs of
students, yet the brief meetings designed to improve the curriculum
proved inadequate. Its largely research-oriented faculty saw the number of candidates for the Ph.D. degree increase each year, yet was
unable to ensure that those candidates indeed developed the research
sophistication needed for a Ph.D. program. The faculty reflected a
number of highly developed talents, yet those talents were too frequently either under or overutilized. It was known that several members from the administrative faculty would retire, but there was little
agreement as to what kinds of replacements should be sought. There
was general accord that there probably should be greater representation of practitioners among the faculty and greater contact with
the field, but converting that awareness to actual specifications for
new appointments exceeded the capabilities of the faculty and the
associated search committees trying to identify candidates for jobs
whose dimensions were unclear. There was in addition frustration

over the quality or effectiveness of examining procedures, the level and intensity of student advisement, the lack of heavy financial support for graduate students, the dysfunctions between faculty research and student needs, and the fact that the faculty was charged with many administrative responsibilities, yet lacked the essential knowledge of community or administrative structure to assume those responsibilities. Before 1969 the committee that existed had functioned in no organized way. Individual faculty members decided on the courses to be taught with little mutual consultation. Committee meetings considered routinely only small administrative details, such as the occasional placement of a graduate, nor did members socialize with each other in any perceivable way. Indeed, the Committee on Administration and Organization Studies was more an aggregate of individuals, each operating as an entrepreneur, than a coherent unit of organization. From 1970 on the committee tried to reorganize and gradually did systematize some processes, but the membership remained dissatisfied with the total educational program. It was out of this sense of frustration that the faculty elected to request funds from the Ford Foundation for an intensive joint student and faculty planning exercise, to consider the curriculum, all other elements of the program, relationships with other schools and departments at Stanford, and relationships with the field. While the faculty voted approval to make such a request and its members agreed to free their calendars for at least a month during the summer of 1973, there was still considerable uncertainty that the effort could produce anything of significance. There was strong suspicion of the school's central administration and many felt that a successful planning effort would simply produce more program expansion without acquisition of needed additional resources. Some felt that while the existing program was far from ideal it still managed to accept students, and to process and place them, and a planning activity might produce something even worse than already existed.

The Summer Workshop

Despite such misgivings, when the Ford Foundation acted favorably on the request for financial support the faculty did agree to spend the month of August attempting to solve some of the vexing problems of the curriculum. The plan was to immerse the entire fac-

ulty, together with a few students, in the problems, in the hope that
this would produce consensus and result in a consistent program. At
a minimum this deep immersion might result in slightly better faculty relationships and an agreement to continue the curricular status
quo. The effort might even produce a new curriculum; conceivably it
could produce a more consistent total program, and perhaps a greater
sense of community on the part of the faculty. The experience might
produce revised courses and procedures which, stated in the form of
guidelines, could help counsel students through the program. It also
could produce new copy for the university catalog and possibly a report that might have some interest off the Stanford campus as well as
on it. The most ambitious hope was to develop a curriculum that
would be visible nationally, which could contribute to general understanding of the education of administrators, and which would signal
an effort on the part of Stanford's administration faculty to assume
national leadership in the training of administrators.

The planning activity made use of a number of techniques which
in aggregate seemed to contribute to reasonably successful outcomes.
None of these techniques, it was clearly recognized, was particularly
new or innovative, but a few of them suggest some principles that
might have general applicability. Each member of the faculty was
asked to prepare a working or position paper about some problem as
background material. Papers were solicited dealing with the possible
core curriculum, admissions policies, field services, joint programs,
community relations, financial support of students, in-service programs for the field, and appropriate degree structures. Curricula from
other schools of education were accumulated as were lists of curricular trends found in the education of educational administrators. Several teams of graduate students conducted opinion surveys of students and alumni, and all this information was provided faculty before the first formal meeting.

The schedule of meetings was structured carefully in advance and
the faculty provided an agenda for each of the four weeks of intensive activity. The first week was intended to focus on a possible core
of required courses and the nature and substance of advanced
courses. The second week focused on relationships with other
schools and departments at Stanford. The third week focused on relationships with the field. The fourth week was to be devoted to a
variety of other details as well as decision-making on the critical mat-

ters the faculty had explored. This structure gave a sense of direction to the conversations, but was not at all restrictive. At the end of each week a summary of the decisions reached was prepared and a new and revised agenda for the following week developed. As the discussions exposed new issues or new opportunities the agenda and summaries reflected these. Yet the overall thrust of the meetings remained faithful to the original design. Of particular significance was the weekly reporting in writing as to unresolved issues and progress made. This seemed to affect morale positively as individuals were able to see that definite progress was being made. As part of the reporting procedure, when it appeared that consensus was being reached on a major policy matter, a policy statement was drafted for reconsideration by the whole faculty. This also provided a sense of forward movement, as well as an opportunity to ensure that everyone agreed on a final policy statement. A serendipitous gain from this process was that much of the composition for the new program description was completed before the workshop ended, allowing for more speedy request for faculty action on the new program.

So that viewpoints other than those of indigenous faculty and students were heard, a judicious use of outside consultants and of faculty elsewhere in Stanford University was undertaken, but care was exercised that consultations were not overpowering. With the exception of one consultant who put in a full week, consultants spent between one and one-half to three hours in meetings altogether. This proved long enough for them to express their opinions while allowing the faculty enough time to consider suggestions in the awareness that it was the faculty itself that would have to live with whatever was decided. Especially valuable were informal meetings with other members of the Stanford faculty who shared their own experiences and reacted to suggestions for the emerging education program and for cooperative efforts with other elements of the university.

For the most part all discussions were plenary in that the full faculty was present. Some small-group and individual efforts were, of course, necessary, but the largest amount of time was spent by the faculty working together as a whole. This seems an especially important way to build mutual respect and a feeling of esprit de corps, although it is potentially hazardous because close proximity over an extended period of time can irritate latent animosities and produce disagreement rather than consensus. In this case that danger was partly guarded against by a decision that four hours of group meeting per day was about all that was tolerable. Inded, the faculty revealed itself to be much more creative in the early hours than during the later hours of even that four-hour period. As a matter of strategy no formal coffee breaks were provided; the group interrupted its four-hour discussions only occasionally, when the spirit moved the faculty. The prolonged coffee hour may have some merits, but the more intensive effort without scheduled breaks seemed more appropriate for the faculty in administration. Its members worked intensively during the mornings, knowing that afternoons would be free for other kinds of work. There were no specially organized social activities except for infrequent lunches when no other time was available to hear a few consultants or resource people. Some argued that the social hour or cocktail hour is an essential ingredient in developing group cohesiveness, but this did not appear to be warranted for the faculty in administration. The sense of affinity or community could flower during the morning work sessions and still allow each individual the privacy of his or her late afternoon or evening time. Given an overcommitted faculty, in retrospect ensuring considerable free and private time for each individual seems to have been one of the essential ingredients.

Conclusion

What the faculty in administration was doing during the summer of 1973 it should properly have been doing throughout the academic year, but the time simply could not be found. Hence the need for the summer work. Payment for that time also seemed essential, to symbolize that what the group was doing was important, to ensure a degree of continuity of effort, and to free faculty members from other commitments to spend the requisite time on the new program. Money in American society does have a tremendously important symbolic value, transcending its use to purchase goods and services. Payment for planning indicates to generally suspicious faculty members that their work is important and is being taken seriously. Payment to student participants seemed equally necessary, and for the same reasons.

Also important was freeing the time of a chairman so that documents could be prepared, summaries composed, agendas revised, and overall reporting take place quickly after events transpired. Freeing the chairman from other obligations and providing him with adequate secretarial help seemed to be an essential condition. Groups can be quite productive and inventive, but they cannot handle the logistical problems of transforming speculation into actual decisions, documents, and new materials. In retrospect, it seems almost axiomatic that such a complex planning activity as this one should not be attempted unless someone is given the freedom of time needed to administer the effort satisfactorily.

Student participation in the process seemed of both substantive and symbolic significance. Looking back, perhaps the symbolic value was more important, because it brought daily reminder that the faculty really was in the business of educating students and that the students did have needs, opinions, and desires that should be considered. Substantively the students played an important reactive role. By constant questioning they forced the faculty to reexamine many of the presuppositions it was making.

Designating the last days as the time for decision-making also proved of value. Listing those times on the agenda became goal setting, and having scheduled time for such discussion meant that responsibility for various matters could be assigned. In preparation for those last two days, the chairman indicated a list of matters that had to be ranked in order of priority along with a list of unfinished business and an outline for a proposed final report. With this documentation in hand the faculty could express its own opinions and, when they were affirmative, individuals could assume specific responsibility. By way of winding up, the chairman listed a number of matters that directly concerned the dean of the School of Education, discussed them with him, and then reported back to the faculty how each item was disposed of. It was this constant reporting back to the faculty, indicating progress, that seemed to be one of the essential ingredients which made the workshop or planning session a relatively successful one.

The long- and short-range outcomes of the planning activity can be indicated, recognizing that considerable work will be necessary before the undertaking can be finally evaluated. A new program was developed and agreed on and there is every indication that the faculty of the School of Education will approve it. Plans have been made for considerable course construction work to go on during academic year 1973-74, but this, of course, depends on the willingness and ability of the faculty members to devote the necessary time to it. Overall, the planning session seemed to have welded the faculty into a cohesive group, loyal to each other and feeling a sense of shared purpose and identity. The mood of the faculty shifted from one of frustration to one of almost exuberant comradeship. As one faculty member remarked, since he had come to Stanford this was the first time he and a group of colleagues had begun to act like a faculty. Divisiveness was eased and individuals became willing to yield even cherished prerogatives and courses for the sake of the program as a whole. What has been produced is the beginning of an administrative unit that has some of the desirable attributes of a department, but lacks the inflexibility and isolation that so often accompanies departmental structure. Whether this will evolve into a truly lasting entity, a viable program, will be determined in the few years immediately following the planning exercise, but the start seemed auspicious.

Notes

1. Dwight R. Ladd, *Change in Educational Policy* (New York: McGraw-Hill, 1970), pp. 197-198.

2. Ibid., p. 200.

3. Summarized from ibid., pp. 200-209.

5. Adaptability

The new program in administration and policy analysis was developed in the School of Education at Stanford with its own unique problems and characteristics in mind, and for that reason we should examine whether or not this particular approach has relevance for other schools of education.

The uniqueness of the program planned for Stanford lies in the strong positive stand that has been taken on a variety of issues, with some of those stands running counter to prevailing tendencies. There is to be a prescribed core of courses required of all students, consuming approximately three-quarters of the first year of graduate work. Some members of the faculty of the School of Education are displeased with such a heavy prescription, especially since the core does not explicitly deal with philosophy, history, psychology, social psychology, the curriculum, or evaluation. But the faculty for administration and policy analysis is persuaded that it understands the needs of future educational administrators and that the prescribed core is the only way to ensure that students are exposed to such materials.

Illustrative of this belief is the fact that the new program will stress quantification through a full year sequence in decision science for all candidates, and a full year of statistics in addition for all Ph.D. candidates. This decision was made in recognition that candidates for degrees in education were probably somewhat less prepared to cope with quantification than candidates in, for example, business, engineering, or the sciences. The faculty is convinced that numerically-based decision-making is so much a part of the future that it states the requirement and will provide remedial work for students whose last contact with mathematics may have been in high school.

Another unique element of the Stanford program is the stress placed on the Ed.D. degree, in opposition to the drift throughout the country toward programs emphasizing the Ph.D. degree. The Ed.D. was originally considered a degree for practitioners but that purpose became contaminated as faculties tried to make the Ed.D. degree more like the Ph.D. The resultant hybrid satisfied neither the needs of practitioners nor the canons of scholarship required in Ph.D. degree programs elsewhere in Stanford University. This fact has probably contributed to the continued lower status accorded schools of education compared with graduate departments in arts and sciences and the older professional schools.

In keeping with this concern for the practitioner is the requirement for paid internships and the willingness on the part of the faculty to devote academic time to administering an internship together with a correlated seminar. In making this recommendation the faculty recognized a tendency for internships generally to regress toward a rather low level of menial work without rigorous supervision. It may be that the new Stanford effort will follow that course. However, there is every intention of devoting sufficient resources to it to ensure the vitality of internships.

Another unique attribute is the serious attempt to make the program genuinely interdisciplinary, interlevel, and interprofessional. The three core courses will be taught by teams of faculty members; each individual of the team represents a different disciplinary background, but has agreed to develop a truly integrated course. The faculty believes that administrators in elementary and secondary education, as well as administrators in higher education, should have a reasonably sophisticated understanding of all levels of education. Hence, the core courses will stress problems and use examples from all levels, and in one of the core sequences actual administrative problems will be given considerable attention. It is assumed that as much as a third of all course work will be taken outside the School of Education, which should further contribute to the interdisciplinary character of the program. The entire program is based in the social sciences; this is the integrating force which it is hoped will unify courses taken in several different fields into a consistent whole. One full year of the core will draw on economics, political science, and sociology, and establish connecting links that students can use to integrate work taken in the School of Business, the Department of Communications, or the School of Law.

A factor that is judged essential but also extremely difficult to accomplish is maintaining the relatively small enrollment in the graduate School of Education with no undergraduate enrollment to offset costs. Stanford is a private university, and while it has substantial endowment must still rely heavily on tuition to support its educational program. The attempts made to generate offsetting income will include opening courses to undergraduates and students elsewhere in the university and a standing master's enrollment if a genuine need exists. However, the stability of maintaining a small program ultimately depends on persuading the central administration of the university that a definite if expensive posture in professional education is appropriate for a private university.

Two other elements unique to the Stanford program should be mentioned. The first is the use of a highly research-oriented faculty to teach practitioners. The entire program is predicated in the belief that this can be done. However, only after the program has recorded considerable history can accurate assessment be made. Secondly, the faculty will offer a Ph.D. degree but will strive to make it clearly a research degree that can exist side by side with a practitioner's degree without invidious comparisons between the two. The Ph.D. degree will require a longer time to complete, more quantification, and will be pursued by a clear minority of students in the program. The Ed.D. degree will be the more typical one, and could ideally come to be equivalent in the School of Education to the MBA offered in the graduate School of Business. In the School of Business the expected and usual program leads to the master's, the Ph.D. being distinctively different and pursued by only a few students aspiring to college teaching positions.

Other schools of education, of course, face different conditions that would affect the appropriateness of the Stanford model. Many have large undergraduate enrollments which provide the financial base but also demand considerable faculty attention and teaching time. Additionally, particularly in publicly supported institutions, schools of education have considerable extension and service responsibilities which, while they provide some opportunities for student work experience, also require substantial faculty travel and sometimes directing faculty energies to service activities rather than to research.

The organizational freedom of schools of education in the public sector is increasingly limited by statewide coordination and control. Schools of education have a tradition of a typical departmental structure which, while it possesses some virtues, does tend to limit the amount of interdisciplinary work that can be undertaken, and state colleges and universities have a larger number of the service professional schools—e.g., social work, recreation, or journalism—than does Stanford. Service-oriented professional schools may have a greater affinity for schools of education, hence a longer tradition of inter-school cooperation, as, for example, the close ties that sometimes exist between a school of education and a school of library science.

Schools of education in publicly supported institutions charge considerably less tuition and their programs are' less dependent on tuition income. This fact in itself seems to allow and even to encourage much greater course and program proliferation. Subspecialties which the Stanford faculty rejects are distinct options for publicly supported programs.

The School of Education at Stanford conceives of having a national and international mission which will determine the nature of the program, recruitment and admissions practices, and placement. The majority of schools of education have a state or regional mission which encourages kinds of program development that would be inappropriate for Stanford.

While such features as those described above can, and very likely will, produce different programs, several features of the Stanford program seem valid for consideration elsewhere. The first is the emphasis on the Ed.D. degree. Schools of education are professional schools whose major mission is the preparation of professional workers. That mission is seriously contaminated by forcing degree candidates into the Ph.D. mold and requiring them to meet criteria developed for a research degree. It now seems likely that the needs of practitioners can most closely be met if a degree is tailored and maintained to provide the educational experiences a future practitioner will require. Secondly, and relatedly, the emphasis on paid internships seems warranted by the experiences of other professional schools and of a few schools of education that have entered into internship work fairly heavily. If a program is developed that requires considerable full-time attendance it is likely that applicants will tend to be younger and more in need of some supervised contact with reality, which other candidates brought with them as they returned to school during the summer to acquire a needed credential.

The emphasis on quantification also seems worth adopting at most places since the emergence of the computer as a powerful tool for administration. So significant is quantification to the Carnegie Commission on Higher Education that it suggests all high school students should be required only to take four years of mathematics and four years of English, everything else being purely elective.

While not all schools of education could limit enrollment as severely as is planned at Stanford, nonetheless smaller-sized doctoral programs would seem to be wise for all schools of education. Not only does there appear to be a declining need for large numbers of credentialed administrators, but also truly rigorous doctoral training seems possible only for small numbers of students interacting intimately with the faculty.

Lastly, the technique of intensive planning for major curriculum revision clearly seems appropriate for adoption elsewhere. The short-term intensive immersion of a faculty in curricular concerns appears more likely to bring about significant change than continuing to allow the normal committee and departmental structures to operate during the regular academic year.

This chapter has been written within the constraints of two assumptions which should at least be questioned. The first assumption is that doctoral degrees are necessary for educational administrators. The School of Education at Stanford offers, and probably will continue to offer, the doctorate for school administrators, largely because credentialing requirements and public opinion demand the doctorate. However, the validity of that demand can be questioned. Graduate schools of business have been highly successful in preparing managers and decision-makers for whom the MBA degree is sufficient. If public attitudes could be reversed, thus restricting the demand for doctoral degrees, perhaps more sharply tailored professional programs in education could be developed.

The second assumption pertains to the number of institutions that properly should be involved in the preparation of educational administrators. If education is truly entering a steady or declining state, the need for credentialed administrators should diminish and, as it does, so should the number of institutions preparing personnel. The faculty of the School of Education at Stanford faced the issue and decided it should continue to prepare administrators, but it could equally as plausibly have reached the opposite conclusion. It is suggested that every school of education similarly question its own purposes, some to arrive at positive and some at negative conclusions.

PART II

TESTING PERCEPTIONS

In January 1974 the School of Education at Stanford conducted an invitational conference to explore new ideas for the preparation of educational administrators and to test some of the judgments which the faculty in administration and policy analysis had made. Three of the major papers from that conference are included here, as well as a summary of briefer statements made by John Dunn, president of Foothill Junior College District; William Cunningham, executive secretary, Association of California School Administrators; Ralph W. Tyler, consultant, Science Research Associates; and Frank Newman, Director of University Relations at Stanford.

6. Education: A Declining or Rising Sun?

H. THOMAS JAMES

As I looked at the topic on which I am to speak tonight, long after I had accepted the invitation to speak, I had some grave misgivings. First, I must confess to a strong and optimistic bias. I believe in education. I believe (if one is stuck with the metaphor) that it is a rising sun, that knowledge and the opportunity for more people to obtain it, are increasing; and that, through rational use and applications of the knowledge that we continue to accumulate, we can improve the human condition. So I come to the first element in my misgiving: The knowledge we are gaining can be rationally applied to good or evil purposes. Perhaps few generations in history have become as conscious as ours of powerful knowledge applied to evil purposes. It follows then that we cannot talk sensibly about education without linking it to morality, thereby seeking to strengthen the ethical framework within which our actions are planned. How to strengthen the ethical framework of our society has become one of the most pervasive concerns of our time, and not one I'm prepared to discuss tonight. All I'm sure of is that education in the broadest sense is essential, and that schooling alone won't do.

As I read the theme of the conference, "Educational Administration in a Steady State," it became obvious that I was not to address the subject of education, which I believe is a rising sun, but the subject of traditional schooling in America, which in some ways probably has passed its zenith. Certainly its relative contribution is declining as other institutions and technologies increase educational services and experiences. Here again I have misgivings because any generalizations about schooling in America usually turn out to be wrong. So to reduce my anxieties about being wrong in this company, I will speak to some very specific aspects of schooling, and specify ways in which I see signs of stability or decline.

The Decline in Numbers to Be Educated

Some of you may recall that I pointed out in an article in *Compact* in 1968 that live births peaked in 1959 at 4.3 million per year, and then declined steadily to 3.5 million, indicating that if births stabilized at that point it would eventually mean a reduction in school enrollments of perhaps 20 percent. Live births have indeed stayed down, and dropped further in 1973 to 3.2 million. They are expected to be lower again this year. Not surprisingly, children who don't get born don't show up in school later! The figure I saw for last year indicated that elementary enrollments were down by 460,000. This loss in enrollment will continue, and will exceed half a million this year. More importantly, it is cumulative and cannot be turned around for at least five years. If live births stay relatively stable at around 3.5 million per year, as they have for the past five years, or decline further, as current estimates suggest they may, the loss of clientele from the schools will indeed approximate 20 percent by the mid-1980s. My plea in the *Compact* article was for planning wise use of the resources released by this decline for the improvement of education, for shifting resources among levels of education, and for extending educational services. I continue the plea, and hope it will be heard more widely than it was in 1968. The dislocations we have already experienced, such as cuts in school staff, a growing oversupply of new teachers, and building shutdowns, are only the leading edge of more massive dislocations to come as schools enter a period of decline in enrollments that will persist certainly through this decade, probably through the next, and perhaps through the turn of the century. To face this decline with gloom, and to let it happen with all its attendant consequences unplanned, seems a mad course to pursue. To seize it as an opportunity to extend educational services, now badly delivered to many age groups and communities, seems to offer the more rational choice, and the one more likely to benefit our society in the long run. The latter course takes massive planning at all levels of government, and some federal funds could be helpful in this task.

Some observers have likened the baby boom following World War II to an ocean wave, and indeed just as we are thrown off-balance when struck by a great Pacific swell, so the educational establishment was caught off-balance in the 1950s and 1960s as rising enrollments pushed up the need for housing, staff, and costs of operation. As we begin to catch our equilibrium at the top of the wave, in the way that we once consistently underestimated the rapid rise in school enrollments, we are now inattentive to the decline setting in, and again may lose our balance. Our teacher training programs were too slow in turning out the teachers needed on the buildup and we were faced with shortages for two decades; now we are too slow in cutting back training programs, and we are faced with an increasing oversupply each year in the number of teachers, administrators, and most kinds of specialists in education. A recent report showed that in 1972-73 24 percent more teachers were certified than teaching positions were available for, and the percentage is sure to be larger this year. In the middle 1960s seven times more administrators were being certified than there were vacancies for, and this year ten times seems a conservative estimate.

As the wave of children that overwhelmed the schools moves on into the world of work, our productive and service institutions doubtless also will be slow to adjust, but we can expect steady and substantial increases in the labor force throughout this decade and into the next that will in turn expand taxable incomes and properties, so that a much larger revenue base will be available for supporting the declining enrollments, with attendant reduction of the individual's burden for the costs of schooling. This is not to say that costs will decrease, for salaries will continue to go up. Furthermore, pupil-teacher ratios will decrease, and this is one of the most power-· ful variables determining cost. However, costs will not increase as fast as they have over the past two decades and the tax base to support the costs will increase much more rapidly. We will need new schools as populations shift, and to replace old buildings, but few for growth.

So while in the 1950s we were unrealistically hopeful about our ability to cope with the problems of education in the 1960s, it seems to me that current discussions in education are unrealistically gloomy about our ability to cope with the problems of the 1970s and 1980s. The worst is over, and if historians show, as I expect them to, that most of the problems of the past decade stemmed from the sheer numbers of students overwhelming our schools, so the decline in those numbers should yield great improvement in the effectiveness of schools in the years ahead. We will be able to reduce the crowding which has raised the anxieties and stirred aggression in students as predictably as it does in experiments on rats, and it should increase the attention that can be given to individuals, for pupil-teacher ratios, which averaged 24.6 pupils per teacher a decade ago, were down to 19.5 in 1972-73; and this in turn should reduce the feeling of anomie, of loss of identity about which we heard so much in the 1960s.

Along with the passing of the postwar wave of children will come other reductions in the costs of social services, for at the same time that this wave was creating problems for schools it was also accelerating our needs for housing and hospitals, doubling the rate of juvenile delinquencies, swamping our custodial institutions, multiplying accidents of all kinds, and in general multiplying the costs of other local government agencies as well as schools. These statistics, too, will soon begin to decline, with predictable stabilization and perhaps reduction ahead for other governmental costs as well. In spite of the dire predictions in the late 1960s about countercultures and revolution, the young people in the leading edge of the wave are now moving into solid and productive adulthood, surprisingly conservative in their views, better educated than the generation they follow, and in general startlingly attractive to their older colleagues who a few years ago were inclined to fear them. I am inclined to conclude that the changing age structure of our population makes the future look much brighter than it seemed only a few years ago.

The Decline in Number of Entry Positions to the Superintendency

Of particular importance to the subject of this conference is the decline in the number of entry positions for the chief administrator of a local school district. Let me personalize the problem.

In 1942, when, at the age of twenty-six, I obtained my first appointment as a superintendent of schools under an elected board, there were over 112,000 school districts in America. Thirty years later, in 1972-73, there were fewer than 17,000. This is not to say that the total number of points of entry to administrative roles has decreased, for minor administrative roles have proliferated enormously as districts grew larger over those three decades. Rather, there is something quite different in the opportunity offered an individual entering administration as the chief administrator under a board of education, even in a small district, from that offered to one appointed by a principal, let us say, to a vice-principalship. In the first instance, from the day he is appointed he deals with the totality of problems of a local school board making public policy for the schools, and if he is bright and reasonably knowledgeable, he deals with them on a basis of equality. His professional peers are in the professional associations he belongs to, and while he may recognize there are differences in the *quantity* of problems dealt with by the superintendent of the largest district among them, he knows there is no difference in the *kind* of problems, and he can, in either his innocence or his wisdom, aspire to that highest position and often achieve it. Quite different is his counterpart in the role of vice-principal. He is excluded by tradition, as most probably is his immediate superior and others in the chain of command above him, from the meetings where public policy is made for the schools, and the potential vacancy chains above him stretch away into distances that appear uncrossable even in the imagination of the most ambitious.

The contrasting roles must have similarly contrasting effects on their incumbents. On the one hand the superintendent in even the small district recognizes that while he deals with a board and learns the essentials of policy formulation and execution, he is making a record visible to other boards who may seek his services. Visibility for the vice-principal is difficult, for his immediate superior is also his chief competitor for promotion, and is therefore not always likely to be helpful in promoting his visibility. In fact there is good reason to believe that Parkinson's law operates in the multiplication of the vice-principal's role because principals prefer to have two assistants, who then tend to compete with each other and not with the principal.

My reasons for emphasizing the difference between a young man entering school administration as superintendent—opportunities that have declined sharply in the last thirty years—and the young man entering the long chain of command of a larger district, should be obvious, but let me try to sharpen them further.

(1) In the first instance, he is involved with the broad sweep of public policy issues from the beginning; in the second, he is involved with complex interpersonal relations and conflicts involving students and staff at a highly personal level, and the administrivia dealing with a narrowly defined subset of the principal's duties.

(2) Even in the microcosm of a small district the superintendent has regular discussions with board and citizens, ranging across the broad sweep of school problems, and his performance record is potentially interesting to other boards. But the vice-principal has a reporting relationship to only one superior, who is primarily interested in seeing that what they discuss goes no further.

(3) The superintendent is in open competition with his peers for other superintendency vacancies, nearby or across the nation, and there is an established procedure for transmitting his record in standardized form. The vice-principal is almost totally dependent on his immediate superior, either for vacating the position or for reporting his qualifications for another.

(4) Finally, the probability is that the one who enters as a superintendent will, because of the broad scope of his functions, be ready for his next job, while the one who enters as a vice-principal will not, because of the narrowness of his first experience.

A Softening of the Rhetoric about Schooling

We have become accustomed over the past two decades to attacks on the schools by the radical right or left, by religious zealots and atheists, racists and integrationists, do-gooders and casual meddlers. Few schools in America can be looked at over time without revealing a succession of what might be called critical incidents or crises. Yet to say the whole system of public education in this country is in need of change is arrant and irresponsible nonsense.

Much of the new money flowing into schools from foundations and from the federal government over the past fifteen years was aimed at producing innovations and changes in the schools, but the statements about the specifics to be changed were oddly incoherent. Schools should be more humane, they should be joyful, and they should be "open." President Johnson gave us program planning budgeting systems, and the Office of Education taught us a new catechism to go with it so their economists could understand what we were doing: decide on objectives, allocate resources to accomplish them, measure the accomplishments, and do cost-benefit studies to see how we can do better next time the cycle comes around. Since the administration changed in 1968, the terms of discourse had to change too, so we have heard little of PPBS since then and more about accountability (whatever that means, and it seems to mean everything or nothing, depending on who's talking). But the catechism is the same—decide on objectives, allocate resources, measure accomplishments, and, through cost-benefit analyses, improve the next cycle. No one can argue with the logic of these proposals. Nor has anyone, to my knowledge, found a sensible way to follow the prescription at the school district level.

Accountability has become one of the most ubiquitous buzz words in education, and happily for all of us its widespread use, as is usually the case with buzz words in education, is probably a signal that it is about to go out of style. I call it a buzz word because it means different things to different people, and for those who seriously try to define the term it fades away as one tries to move closer to its meaning. At its best it appears to mean that schools should define their tasks, and report on how well those tasks are achieved. At its worst it seems to depend on pupil performance on achievement tests, and to serve the general expectation of parents that all children should be above average. Yet behind accountability lies a deep concern that schools serve children well (in a large number of poorly specified ways); that they be orderly in setting their goals and measuring their achievements; that they be responsive to the diverse demands of their many constituencies; and that all these things be done in ways that build public trust. This is a large order, perhaps too large for an institution like the school, which was standardized long ago, because the diversity of demands made on it by the very diverse subpopulations it serves makes virtually impossible a clear statement of goals and clear standards for performance.

Changes we have had in schools, as a result of great pressures over the past decade, and unquestionably more are needed. Yet not all changes being proposed are needed in all schools, and so proposals for universal change are nonsensical. A school mirrors the community it serves and changes only in response to the expectations of the community it serves. Change is a two-sided coin; its other side is *stability*. The lesson to be learned from our experience with the federal and foundation money directed to changing the schools is that as long as we have local boards of education the money will be used to satisfy local expectations, which may lead either to changes satisfactory to them or to stabilizing or extending existing services. In communities where other institutions, like the family, the churches, local government, etc., work well, the schools work well; where other institutions are failing, the schools are failing; and no amounts of money have been able to change that equation. Further, we are well into a remarkable period in the history of schooling in which we are establishing procedures for a broad spectrum of decisions that traditionally were made on an ad hoc basis, in such areas as teachers' rights, student rights, conditions of work, quality of service, etc. The development of these procedures can be expected to increase stability, redistribute power, and modify the rights and responsibilities of boards, administrators, teachers, students, and citizens generally.

Instead of crying for unspecified innovation and change across all schools, we need to capitalize on the great potential for stability in the schools. As we become increasingly specific about establishing procedures we will increase the ability of school boards and administrators, teachers, pupils, and citizens to introduce in orderly ways the specific changes needed in specific schools to meet the expectations of specific communities, while at the same time recognizing and mediating the pressures from state and national governments that reflect our societal commitment to racial justice and quality education. As we build procedural order we may also find ways to recognize and perhaps integrate the educational experiences offered by other institutions, capitalizing on them where they are robust and positive, strengthening them where they are weak or negative.

We have been bombarded in recent years with the assertion that schools aren't very important. This notion, influential in the last century, has been given new life in the past decade by romantic writers like Ivan Illich. Certain interpretations of such research findings as Coleman's and Jencks's are again making this notion particularly compelling. Yet Illich's proposal for deschooling society is less revolutionary than would be the society he hopes would emerge, which is one with sharply lowered expectations for material, technical, and spatial comforts. No such society would be acceptable to even a small percentage of our people. Even the 100,000 alienated middle-class youth of the sixties, who have dropped out to form the 3,000 "new life-style communities" scattered across the country, are unlikely to persist, except where powerful religious conversion is involved. Schools continue to perform their traditional function of escalating children up through the socioeconomic classes, and few among the lower levels and deprived minorities are confused by either romantic talk or plausible research. The socioeconomic escalator runs two ways, and those among the children of the upper and middle class who choose to drop out provide the counterflow that makes room at the top for children of the lower socioeconomic groups who persist with their education. We live in a vastly complex technological society with insatiable demands for knowledgeable people to keep it running, and with an overwhelming majority dedicated to keeping it running, out of which will come the inventions and adaptations and the energy to keep it running and improve it. If the reservoirs of middle- and upper-middle-class children who were expected to run it reject the discipline and refuse to achieve the knowledge necessary, another reservoir will be tapped and the hard-working children of blue-collar parents and less privileged ethnic groups will be gathered into the roles of the new elite. Revolution we may have, but not the kind of violent revolution talked about by present-day romantics; rather its progress will be marked by the orderly selection of qualified people, whatever their background, who will make the adaptations, invent the new technologies, and find the energy sources we need. The school in this function is performing well the task that was dreamed for it when state school systems were first established in our country.

The Persistence of Our Faith in Schooling

That our faith in schooling is strong in spite of years of romantic and radical attacks on it is revealed by the fifth annual Gallup poll of public attitudes toward education, published in the September 1973 *Phi Delta Kappan.* To the question, Do you think your child is learning what you believe should be learned? 82 percent said yes. To the question, Does your child go to school because he wants to or because he is required to? 83 percent said because he wants to. To the question, How important are schools to one's future success? 95 percent answered extremely important to fairly important. On whether children were getting a better education than those questioned had received, 61 percent of the total said better, and of those who were parents of children in public schools, 69 percent said better. Asked what the biggest problems in schools are now, the top three mentioned were lack of discipline, integration-segregation conflicts, and lack of financial support. Asked what makes today's education better, the top three replies listed in order (1) better curriculum, (2) better facilities, and (3) better-qualified teachers.

Reading these responses, it is hard to feel that the schools are in crisis or out of favor with the public. Read one way, it would seem more reasonable to say that the faith of our people in schooling is strong, and the future looks better to us than it did in the sixties. Read another way, one can find it disturbing, for it reveals no sensitivity to the expanding role of other institutions in the education of youth, a point I will return to later.

The Persistence of Knowledge Gained from Schooling

Lest someone suggest that faith in schooling is not enough, we recently obtained some hard data on one question about schooling that certainly seems important. Schooling is supposed to increase knowledge. The question asked by Professor Herbert Hyman of Wesleyan University was: What evidence can we find in surveys of the adult population that additional years of schooling add to the knowledge of adults, and how long does such knowledge endure? He sought his answers in a secondary analysis of surveys of large and representative samples of the national population over the past twenty years, extracting from them the data needed to answer these questions. He found not a single instance where the college graduates are not the most knowledgeable group, not a single instance where high school graduates were not less knowledgeable than the college group, nor more knowledgeable than the elementary group. Furthermore, any waning of the effects of education in old age never goes so far as to reverse or even equalize the superiority of knowledge of the better educated group. Finally, Professor Hyman concludes that in our high schools, and even more so in our colleges, the information-gathering habits gained lead graduates to search for and accumulate new knowledge. Thus while the differences persist, sharp and distinct, among those who stop with elementary school, high school graduates, and college graduates, over time the level of knowledge is rising at all levels, and the old dream of a learning society may no longer be as impossible as it once seemed. So to the extent that we are concerned about the knowledge implanted by schooling, the faith indicated by the polls seems to be justified by Professor Hyman's research, a reassurance for the present and a source of new hope for the future.

The Persistence and Stability of Our Traditional Values in Education

One can look at values as expressed in early American statements about schooling and perhaps despair that our traditional values are fading. Yet it is easy to overlook the fact that the terms that were used in those earlier days are transformed into new terms which yet convey the old meanings.

The concern for piety meant that children must be taught to read in order to study the Bible and grow in religious faith, spiritual-mindedness, temperance, purity, righteousness, and charity, and thereby join the elect, those to be saved after death, the children of God.

The concern for civility involved teaching of good manners and deportment, prudence, courtesy and thoughtfulness, gentleness, tolerance, and graciousness toward others.

Educational writings of the eighteenth century reflected the growing impact of the Enlightenment on the popular consciousness. Piety, secularized, became "virtue"; the concept of civility became "citizenship," reflecting a growing interest in the political philosophers who thought the importance of education lay in its development of the capacity for self-government (a proposition now somewhat in doubt); and more emphasis was placed on knowledge considered scientifically and morally useful. The Northwest Ordinance of 1787 combines the earlier aims of seventeenth-century education and the new emphasis of the eighteenth in its opening words: "Religion, morality, and knowledge being necessary to good government, schools, and the means of education, shall be forever encouraged."

The concern for morality persisted as part of the curriculum throughout the eighteenth century and late into the nineteenth.

Many have worried for fear that in this century these concerns have gone dormant, and expressed the hope that a reawakening will soon be apparent and effective. The signs that some kind of a reawakening of concern for moral education in our schools is imminent are increasingly abundant, and may well become a priority for schools in this decade. Professor Lawrence Kohlberg of Harvard University is giving early leadership to the effort. Perhaps we may find or invent an approach more profound and less controversial than the *McGuffey's Readers* of the last century.

The Industrial Revolution created a new expectation for the schools, that is, that they teach children to be productive. With its connotations of fruitfulness, creativity and ingenuity, gainful employment and investment, productivity is perhaps best epitomized in the Morrill Act of 1862 establishing the land grant colleges, and in succeeding efforts to encourage vocational education and manpower training that have continued up to the present congressional deliberations. In the Gallup poll mentioned earlier 90 percent of the respondents said schools should give more emphasis to a study of trades, professions, and business to help students decide on their careers.

Our own century continues to use and develop the aims of the past. Piety, virtue, or "ethics," implying the effort to find a moral basis for action, is still a broadly recognized value today. Certainly the old concept of civility is still with us, if evidenced only by the persistent cries for its restoration to discourse, procedures, and relationships in the present. We still promote as a goal the pursuit of knowledge, the intellectual or "cognitive" aspects of education, adding to this a concern—perhaps new, perhaps only a version of piety and civility—for the capacity to feel and to empathize. Our concern for good citizenship and self-government is, if anything, stronger than ever before.

In some ways the old aims are adapting to a new world. Citizenship is reaching out from narrow community concerns to a deeper national and international consciousness. We have a new awareness of the environmental consequences of our actions, and the limitations of resources once thought to be inexhaustible. Although the concern for productivity persists, broadened in our own century by a balancing concern for rational consumption and worthy use of leisure time, in light of our population growth and other economic, social, and natural changes, it must be nearing a major transformation. At least young voices of dissent have been telling those who would listen, and the energy crisis has informed those who can see and feel. Our curricular choices in the last two decades show a deeper concern for justice in the distribution of social and economic benefits than before, and judging from our recent graduates the lessons have been well learned, for a new generation is emerging from our schools ready to wrestle with institutionalized irresponsibility. In these days there seems to be a special need above all to teach hope, for in this virtue many of our current graduates seem somewhat deficient.

These are some of the traditional aims of education in our society, along with some speculation on those emerging. I think no one can seriously argue that any of the concepts is irrelevant in our time. One can argue that they are global concepts derived from philosophy and religion, and therefore of little use in an age that seeks to define its educational objectives in behavioral terms. My reply would be that these aims do describe behaviors—how a human being treats his neighbors, the actions he takes part in and approves, what he initiates in his own life. It was with these aims for education in mind that state legislatures established our state school systems throughout the nineteenth century and into the twentieth. More important, it is in terms of these aims that the larger controversies and criticisms of the schools are still phrased. We can stir national concern about how Johnny can't read, but when citizens meet in their local communities to discuss the problem, the discussion shifts to Johnny's behavior, his dress, the length of his hair, his morals, his religious attitudes, his values, and what he's thinking of doing with his life. And it is in terms of these aims that the school leaders, their programs, the faculties, and the students of the foreseeable future will be judged, if we continue to view our schools as they were viewed in the last century and through much of this one.

My final point I make with the gravest misgivings, for I feel that we must abandon the nineteenth century notion that schools alone can accomplish the aims of education. We must also abandon the corollary, that schools can be judged by the degree to which the aims of education are accomplished. Schools alone cannot accomplish the aims of education that we have defined for ourselves in this society. They are necessary, and so we will continue to support them, but they are not sufficient. If we have learned anything from the efforts to change the schools in the past two decades, we should now know that schools work best in communities where all our other institutions work best, including the family, the churches, the many voluntary service associations, the libraries, all the media, local government, and others. In communities where some or all of the other institutions are failing, the greatest effort to improve the functioning of schools will not accomplish the aims of education defined by the larger society.

So I close as I began, optimistic about the rising sun of education, convinced that schooling is necessary, but also convinced that we must abandon our nineteenth-century notion that schools are the only instrument the society has to accomplish its aims for education. Somehow, if schoolmen are to be educators, they must learn more about how all our institutions interact, and about the necessary and sufficient conditions under which this interaction can maximize the achievement of our aims for education.

7. *Commitment and Competence in Educational Administration*

JAMES G. MARCH

Every sermon must have a text. I take mine from a book by J. Jean Hecht:

> If we chart the relative size of occupational groups in mid-twentieth century America, educators would undoubtedly rank with the largest. A variety of economic developments and resulting social changes created a steadily increasing demand for educators; multiple sources furnished a constantly increasing, though generally inadequate, supply.
> . . . Upward mobile Americans, fully alive to the value of an education as a symbol of success, took care that their children's educations were no less extensive than those of the traditional social elite. . . . For the established middle class the importance of a good education was greatly intensified by this challenge from the upward mobile. . . . The earlier dictum that an education ought to be no more extensive than was demanded by a person's job gave way completely to the rule that it should be as extensive as his fortune would permit. . . . Educators came from social levels as diverse as the professions and the rural poor; many

sections of the population were represented in the ranks of teachers and administrators. . . . The principal motives that sent members of different social classes into educational occupations were a desire for security and the desire to rise in the economic and social scale. Educational institutions were both a refuge and a means whereby improved social status could be attained. As a refuge, they chiefly benefited women. . . . Thus one author remarks: "The general course for young women is to go into teaching." . . . To the children of working men, clerks, and farmers, teaching and educational administration had appeal because they meant the possibility of substantial pecuniary rewards and the possibility of upward mobility. . . . Since these chances were most fully realized by educators who held administrative posts in middle class communities, such positions were the most coveted. . . . They were occupied mostly by men. . . . Viewed in the context of mid-twentieth century American society, educators had special significance. They were important agents in the process of cultural change.[1]

Such a description might be faulted, but as a background to educational institutions in the last part of the century, it seems accurate enough. The accuracy, however, is instructive; the description was actually written to describe a different social institution in a different historical era. I have altered a few words. Professor Hecht wrote not about teachers and educational administrators in twentieth century America, but about domestic servants in eighteenth century England.

Domestic service in the eighteenth century had many parallels with educational institutions in the twentieth:

- It involved a substantial part of the population.
- It provided a major avenue for social mobility.
- It was a conduit for the diffusion of beliefs, styles of behavior, and moral codes.
- It was a major symbol of success.
- It was seen as an indispensable institution for society.
- It was the subject of considerable social commentary.

Despite the significance of domestic service to the social structure of eighteenth-century England, it no longer exists as an important social institution. There was no easily identified dramatic event that changed the position of domestic service, it simply went into a decline. Twentieth-century American schools are important social institutions also, and they seem likely to drift into a similar state of archaic curiosity.

The viewpoint is not cataclysmic. I assume the American educational apparatus will change gradually over time, but that educational institutions approximately as we know them will persist for some time to come. There will be schools, school districts, and colleges. I assume that the activities of administrators will be modified in the future, but that recognizably administrative roles will continue to exist in recognizably bureaucratic organizations for some time to come. Tomorrow, I fear, will be something like today, even as today is remarkably like yesterday. The changes of the next two decades are mostly those that are already certain in the simple logic of ordinary demography, economics, and politics.

In a longer perspective, moreover, education as an *activity* will doubtless continue, just as food preparation and shelter maintenance have continued. But our system of classrooms, teachers, and principals is dying, just as the system of pantries, parlor maids, and butlers died. In the long run, what we will ask of our leaders is not whether they were successful in keeping educational institutions alive, but whether they helped them to die with grace, dignity, and intelligence.

Education in Decline

Education is a declining industry. We have apparently entered the third natural phase in the history of a social institution. The first stage is a period of dynamic growth. Social expectations rise; the institution is able to meet those expectations; there is excitement, expansion, and self-confidence. The second stage is a period of conflict. In the period of neglect social expectations outrun capabilities. Social expectations decline; the institution remains able to meet many of the reduced expectations; there is indifference, passivity, and stagnation.

During the first two phases of the life-cycle, we seem to have generated significant elements of superstition in our beliefs about education. During the period of growth, most problems seemed to have many good solutions. Educational administrators, their teachers, and their audiences came to believe that they had figured out what it took to make a successful school. Since many different things worked about equally well, different schools of experts arose. Each was subjectively confident; each was able to cite experience in support of his self-confidence.

During the period of conflict, the half-life of a problem was forever. No matter what we did, the problems persisted. Administrators, their teachers, and their audiences kept looking for the solution without finding it. Schools of education, foundations, and governmental agencies kept supporting solutions, abandoning one for another without changing their luck.

The move from a period of conflict to a period of neglect is not a happy move. As long as our social problems appeared to be solvable and were being solved, educational leaders did not resist taking responsibility for the success. Much of the growth of our educational establishment was rationalized in terms of the contribution of educational institutions to everything from prosperity to social progress to moral reform.

Now we are not so sure. Failure has led to a recognition of the limits of responsibility. Our conspicuous failures, in combination with the retreat from claims of responsibility, will almost certainly reduce the demands on schools over the coming few years. Social expectations adapt to social beliefs about the capabilities of institutions. As a result, the social pressure on schools is likely to decline. That does not make the context much better. Indifference is different from hostility, but it is not a less constraining administrative position. The educational establishment will have to pay the price for having persuaded society that institutionalized education is not a general solution to social ailments. Managers who have become adept at dealing with confrontation will have to adapt to a world in which the audience is small. Those who have only recently embraced external conflict management as the fundamental fact of administration will discover the conflict muted by ennui.

The Characteristics of a Declining State

A declining institution has certain regular administrative characteristics. Leadership tends to age. This is particularly true when decline follows a period of rapid growth. Leadership is relatively young in the wake of promotion and mobility during the growth period. It is then locked into place by lack of opportunities. A high rate of turnover can be sustained only by an increase in involuntary exits. Although some such increase is likely in schools, we can expect a gradual aging of personnel over the next decade.

At the same time, decline produces a loss of joy and an oversupply of qualified professionals. There are fewer chances for advancement. There are fewer resources. There are fewer occasions of success. The process by which teachers and administrators are recruited and trained is not controlled enough to avoid a large number of newly qualified professionals at a time of lessened demand for their services. The result is a backlog of trained people doing other things. Such a backlog simultaneously reduces enthusiasm and increases pressure on educational organizations to provide career opportunities by inventing more bureaucratic superstructure.

Although resources do not necessarily decline in absolute terms, there is a decrease relative to the demand for them within the institution. This eliminates resource buffers between contending groups in the institution. Internal conflict becomes overt, and the organization has little experience in dealing with it. The rules of consensus or executive wheeling and dealing that worked well earlier seem to be less effective in maintaining or moving the institution. Innovation and change through the classic growth techniques of incremental additions and resource bribery become less feasible.

Although the major shock of discovery should pass shortly, the reality of decline is likely to persist for some time. As time passes, the natural processes of institutional adaptation will ameliorate some of the symptoms of decline. Aspirations will be scaled down to feasible levels. Ambitious employees will leave or find another outlet for their ambitions. People in the organization will grow accustomed to quiet irrelevance.

As a result of decline, educational administration in the next decade will face a different context from educational administration of the past decade. Although that context appears in many ways unattractive, it has some positive sides. Educational bureaucracies, like others, suffer from the ailments of growth: simple waste; the transformation of self-interest into self-indulgence; the easy acceptance of convenient fictions. Although it is possible to overstate the case, it is certainly true that adversity has a potential for bringing some semblance of simple efficiency, some discovery of collective coherence, some reexamination of self-comforting dogmas. Decline will make personal success less easy and heroic glory less likely, but it is a time in which certain kinds of administrative creativity can thrive.

The opportunities for change provide a thread of optimism in the cloth of organizational discouragement. The opportunities are real. The decline of the 1930s was a period of considerable ferment in some American educational institutions; the decline of the 1970s may be similar. But we ought not to base our commitment to educational institutions solely on the possibilities for a new birth of creative vigor. Declining institutions need leadership too. Geriatrics is as important in administration as it is in medicine.

The Limits in What Can Be Done

The context of decline demands humility from educational leaders, a sentiment that wisdom might have encouraged earlier, but necessity imposes now. In particular, we need to acknowledge two kinds of limitations on managerial heroics: (1) the limits of human control over human destiny; and (2) the limits of personal incentives as motives of individual behavior. The limitations are not unique to times of decline, but they become more obvious then. They challenge some precious axioms of organizational life. They modify our metaphors of leadership.

First, *limits of human control.* We need to be wary of the ideology of administration. That ideology includes the belief that:

> If there is a problem there is a solution. If there is a solution it is discoverable through analysis, and implementable through skill in interpersonal relations. The discovery and implementation of solutions are duties of the administrator. If a problem persists, it is due to inadequacy in an administrator's will, perception of problems, analysis, or skill with people.

The ideology is attractive in some ways. It comprises a faith of hope. It encourages persistence in the face of adversity. But it is also a basis for self-deception or disillusion. The existence of a problem does not imply the existence of a solution. It is quite possible, and certainly consistent with experience, that problems do not have solutions. There are many solutions that cannot be implemented. Conflict is sometimes real and not susceptible to "resolution." The complexity of implementation may considerably outrun the complexity of the solution or the capabilities of participants. Problems persist for many reasons that have nothing to do with an administrator. In fact, his contribution to the existence or elimination of problems is usually exaggerated. All of these complications are significant to educational institutions. We have problems without solutions; root causes without means of affecting them; solutions without capability of using them.

The implications are conservative. We should have only modest hope that a change in administrator behavior will solve the problems of modern education. Those problems respond to many factors; only a small proportion of them are amenable to administrative control. We need a style that is pessimistic about great drama, but insistent on the necessity for making marginal improvements that are perceptible. We need a perspective on human limits that allows playful relaxation from the coercion of self-importance. We need administrative optimism that is based not on hope for success but on the necessity of moral action.

Second, *the limits of personal incentive.* We are often inclined to believe that modern society and its institutions are powered by personal incentive. The basis of action is ambition. The foundation of administration is the administrative career. The point to a career is the certification of success. We know we are a success in one job by virtue of our promotion to another. When careers become doubtful or unattractive, much of the ambition theory of administration is undermined. This is particularly true in an organization in which there are no direct measures of administrative performance.

As concepts in a theory of administrative behavior, personal incentive and self-interest provide less predictive power than we seem to think, and will provide even less in the future. As concepts in a philosophy of administration, they provide inadequate guides to action, and even more inadequate ones for the future.

According to a personal incentive theory, one acts because of the consequences of his actions. I do what I do because it leads to attractive consequences (e.g., success, or other virtuous things). We justify (or explain) behavior in terms of its consequences. Such an understanding of behavior is important, but is only one of several alternative procedures for justification. For example:

- I do what I do because of my experiences in life.
- I do what I do because others do it.
- I do what I do because of God's will.
- I do what I do because it is what is appropriate.

The last of these is particularly important to administration. Roles in organizations impose obligations on people. Those obligations are (and ought to be) met, not necessarily because they have attractive consequences in terms of either personal ambition or current awareness of personal or organizational objectives, but because that is the duty of the role. When we attempt to fit all human behavior into the incentive mode, we ignore such things. As a result, we err.

This is true when we try to manage the behavior of others. Administrative history is filled with the failures of incentive strategies for producing change. It is also true when we attempt to understand and improve our own behavior. I think we need to realize that our ideology tends systematically to glorify self-interest and its moral corollary of freedom and to underestimate the virtues and pleasures of duty, obligation, and dependence.

Commitment and Competence

Contemporary educational administration requires competence more than heroics, and commitment more than ambition: commitment to persist without serious expectation of either victory or glory, competence to do well the difficult minor things that can be done.

Securing commitment will not be easy. We have grown accustomed to the idea that good administrative work is rewarded by clear success, social approval, and personal promotion, preferably within a few years. Such a perspective is awkward in a decline. Our proper hero is Don Quixote de la Mancha, not Henry Ford.

Securing competence is not trivial either. The glamor of Napoleonic charisma tends to obscure the reality of Napoleonic attention to supplies. It is difficult to keep the toilets in repair, but serious administrative leadership begins there.

I think it is possible to identify some things that are important to modern administrative competence. Consider, for example, the following five analytical skills:

(1) *The analysis of expertise:* The management of knowledge. Much administration involves managing the relation between the expert and the nonexpert, the taking and giving of advice. Administrators deal with experts, and are experts. They give advice and they take it. Both aspects are important. Indeed, both are important in a single relationship.

(2) *The analysis of coalitions:* The management of conflict. Different individuals and groups bring different interests and objectives to the organization. The interests vary in their mutual compatibility partly as a consequence of the form they take, but also partly as a consequence of the alternative combinations of policies and options that are provided. An educational manager is a builder of political coalitions.

(3) *The analysis of ambiguity:* The management of goals. Educational administrators are involved in decision-making under ambiguity. That is, not only are they uncertain about the consequences of alternatives, they are also unclear about their goals, uncertain of their technology, and unaware of their alternatives. They need to be able to act intelligently in the absence of clear objectives.

(4) *The analysis of time:* The management of attention. Educational administrators, like other managers, operate under time constraints. Time and attention are scarce goods. As a result, the procedures by which time is allocated are of some significance to the management of an enterprise. Recent research has indicated that many administrators (including those in education) have the subjective sense that their time is badly allocated.

(5) *The analysis of information:* The management of inference. Decision-making in education involves data. There are data; the data are often relevant to some decision; they are usually incomplete or subject to some error or indecisive; as a result, they require some kind of inferential judgment.

None of these skills will reverse the main trends of educational history. Rather, each is linked to the everyday requirements of managerial competence. Each is also clearly an intellective skill. Each involves a technology of analysis and thought. Each is based on the intellectual development of a scheme of analysis. Each is currently incomplete in development. Each demands a program of research as well as a program of training, testing, and redesign.

The task is large enough to occupy our talents for a long time. The intellectual challenge is significant; the technical demands are impressive. If we develop techniques and training that improve our capabilities to deal with experts, to act intelligently in the absence of goals, to treat data from a decision perspective, to manage conflict and coalitions, and to allocate time, it will be an impressive set of contributions. We will not change the fundamental course of major events, but we will make the marginal improvements in competence that make life somewhat better.

Note

1. J. Jean Hecht, *The Domestic Servant Class in the Eighteenth Century* (London: Routledge & Kegan Paul, 1956), pp. 1, 2, 19, 20, 23, 38, 41, 63, 200. The original text reads as follows:

> Were it possible to chart accurately the relative size of occupational groups in eighteenth-century England, the servant class would undoubtedly rank with the largest. A variety of economic developments and resulting social changes created a steadily increasing demand for domestics throughout the period; multiple sources furnished a constantly increasing, though generally inadequate, supply. . . . Fully alive to the value of a large complement of domestics as a symbol of wealth, the wealthy merchants also took care that their establishments were no less extensive than those maintained by the nobility and gentry. . . . For the nobility and gentry the importance of maintaining a numerous train of servants was greatly intensified by this challenge from the middle class. . . . The medieval dictum that an establishment ought to be no larger than demanded by its master's social status gave way completely to the rule that it should be as extensive as his fortune would permit. . . . The servant class, then, was composed of recruits from social levels as diverse as the gentry and the rural proletariat; many sections of the population were represented in its ranks. . . . The principal motives that sent members of these different classes into service were the desire for security and the desire to rise in the economic and social scale. Service was both a refuge and a means whereby improved social status could be attained. As a refuge it chief-

ly benefited women. . . . Thus, Sir John Fielding remarks: ". . . the general resource of young women is to go to service" . . . . To the daughters of tradesmen as well as to the sons of cottagers, then, service had an appeal because it meant the possibility of substantial pecuniary rewards and the possibility of social elevation. . . . Since these chances were most fully realized by servants who held higher posts in upper-class families, such positions were the most coveted. . . . At the top of the servant hierarchy was the land steward. . . . The house steward was a man of slighter stature. . . . The housekeeper . . . served under him, acting as his assistant. . . . Viewed in the context of eighteenth-century English society, the domestic servant class has a special significance. It was an important agent in the process of cultural change.

8. Enriching Educational Administration as a Field of Study

JAMES A. KELLY

The theme of this conference suggests that the study and practice of educational administration may be significantly altered in the coming decades by recent declines in economic support and in pupil enrollments. There are important respects in which educational administration at any point in time will be heavily influenced by contemporaneous social, economic, racial, religious, and political circumstances. Education is, after all, always a conservative process, more a reflection of predominant social values than an independent initiator of new trends. The current rate of decline in elementary and secondary school enrollments, almost one million fewer pupils each year, will certainly have serious repercussions both in school systems and in schools of education. It is to Stanford's credit that they ask outsiders to join them in the process of developing a response to these changing conditions.

I would like to identify briefly two dimensions of thought—law and political philosophy—that will have to be included in the repertory of perspectives about educational administration, and which have not been extensively discussed by previous speakers. First, however, I want to discuss some conceptions of administration that are useful regardless of social circumstance, and to focus on one in particular—decision-making—in a way that can bridge the gaps that frequently appear between scholars and practitioners of administration.

Scholars and administrators hold a variety of apparently contradictory and frequently overlapping conceptions of what educational administration really is. A complex social function can never be adequately described and explained by a simple or single definition to which allegiance shall be expected from all. In some settings and for some purposes one conception is useful, while other circumstances require a different conception. An effective educational administrator needs to have a repertory of appropriate constructs and an understanding of the conditions in which the use of each of them is appropriate.

Three conceptions of administration deserve noting: administration as *leadership,* as *resource allocation,* and as *mediation of competing political demands.* Then I will discuss two concepts central to all that administrators do: the concepts of *decision-making* and *hypothesizing.*

It could be said that Plato was the earliest writer to view leadership as the primary function of administration. In *The Republic* and in his dialogues, Plato argued that only a very small number of persons could attain sufficient intellectual prowess to understand "truth," and that these philosophers should be placed in positions of great authority over lesser men. Indeed, he urged that philosopher-kings would make the most effective rulers—an idea not totally alien to our exaltation of the status and creature comforts due senior administrators.

It is not for us to trace the influence of Plato's thinking through the centuries, but it is important to note the significance attached in twentieth-century administrative literature to the concept of leadership. Elwood P. Cubberley's classic text, *Public School Administration,* pictured the school administrator in heroic terms as chief executive, the "eyes, and ears, and brains" of the school board. Cubberley saw the administrator as generalist—the center and source of authority, direction, and even inspiration for the schools he "ran."

An excellent example of the way leadership is thought to be central to the essence of administration is the schoolman's tradition that "the principal is the instructional leader of the school." Several generations of school principals assumed that instructional leadership is their primary mission.

More recently some have distinguished between administration and leadership, defining administration as the maintenance of an organization's existing goals and procedures, and leadership as initiation of a new structure or procedure for changing an organization's goals and objectives.

A second conception of educational administration calls attention to the administrator's function as resource allocator. Large, complex organizations like public school districts and state education agencies require staff, supplies, equipment, space, time, and other resources. Indeed, one oversimplified description of administration is to say it is the management of money, people, and things.

In recent years educational administrators increasingly have been drawn into resource allocation problems by two new (at least new to public education) developments: collective bargaining and cost-effectiveness analysis. Collective bargaining agreements between boards and teachers touch on all aspects of resource allocation and school operations; the contemporary school resource allocator must know much more about labor-management relations than did administrators of a previous generation.

Similarly, methods of comparing costs and benefits of educational programs, sometimes called cost-effectiveness analysis, are widely discussed as a potentially significant tool of school management. Because demands for public services always exceed the resources available to the public sector, schools compete with other public services for the tax dollar; within education itself various levels and programs compete with each other for scarce resources. Both citizen and educator will increasingly rely on cost-effectiveness studies to support arguments for particular educational activities. The difficulties they will encounter, however, are formidable. Goals are unclear, and when clear are not always quantifiable. The methodology needed to establish cause and effect is more fragile than most purveyors of cost-benefit rhetoric understand.

Caught between many constraints—students, citizens, teachers, resources, governments, laws, habits—the educational administrator who bases his decisions solely on his own professional judgment is rare indeed. More often the administrator, relying where he can on his private convictions, attempts to reconcile the competing demands that are made on him and arrive at a decision acceptable to many if not enthusiastically supported by all. Politics is the process by which such demands are expressed, aggregated, processed by those with decision-making authority, and announced as policy.

It can be seen that this conception places the educational administrator at the heart of a never-ending political process between community and educational institution. Managing this political process effectively is one of the major challenges facing educational administrators during the 1970s. That it could be managed better during the next decade than it was during the last should not require elaboration for the citizen or educator aware of the turbulence and truculence of school-community, board-employee, and parent-teacher relationships during the 1960s. This also implies that school administrators must possess the social process skills to enable them to help knowledgeable people function together successfully.

Decisions

There are many substantive conceptions of educational administration. Each conception can be thought of as an area of content important both to the study and to the practice of administration. The areas differ with respect to the substance, the content, the subject matter to which administration relates. They are dimensions of administration, frames of reference, somewhat artificially sliced out of the richness of the actual administrative situation to facilitate the analysis of administration.

Administration always involves *choices*, sometimes irreconcilable choices: among alternative ways of allocating resources, among various ways to organize a social process, among political demands, among styles of leadership, and among choices of values to pursue. A distinctive characteristic of administering an enterprise, as distinguished from other roles, is that one is constantly confronted with choices that have both value and factual content, and are *consequential* to the enterprise as a whole and to the persons whose lives are touched by the enterprise. This interaction with choice is at the heart of the process of administration.

There are innumerable possible ways to describe this process of choosing. Let us describe the process of making consequential choices about an enterprise by the term, *decision-making*.

Let it be said at the outset that decision-making in educational administration is not a precise science. As a matter of fact, it is so imprecise that many educational administrators frankly claim that what they practice is art, not science. They stress the intangibles, the values, the unknowns, the guesswork, the human frailties, which pervade decision-making in educational administration. They discount the likelihood that the social and behavioral sciences can break out of the laboratory and make their theories relevant to the "real" world in which administration is practiced. They stress the importance of practical experience to successful administration and rely heavily in their own careers on the lessons they learned as young apprentices, learning their trade by simple observation, word-of-mouth testimony, and trial and error. Finally, they emphasize that all important decisions about education have serious value implications which cannot be resolved by social science.

There *are* severe shortcomings in the capacity of present-day social science that must be understood by educational decision-makers and other users of social science.

It is likely that society's leaders one hundred years from now will look back on twentieth-century social and behavioral science techniques as primitive and clumsy tools. The list of limitations on the efficacy of social science is lengthy. Consider, for example, two problems that have implications for administrators. First, it appears that most social phenomena, such as educational decision-making, have both multiple causes and multiple effects. The ties that link a single event to all its causes and effects are only dimly understood today; the process by which such understanding is advanced is likely to be slow. Current social science methodology is extremely limited in its capacity to establish clear cause-effect relationships; only experimental research designs and theories backed by substantial evidence can claim the power to identify cause-effect patterns.

A second basic problem is that social science shoots at a moving target: human behavior. While there are universalistic dimensions of behavior that probably remain fairly constant over time and among various cultures and nations, there are clearly many ways in which behavior is distinctive in different cultures and at different times. This problem is not apparent in physical and biological sciences, where phenomena such as gravity, photosynthesis, and reproduction are quite constant from one place to another and from one year to the next. Not so with many social science problems. The successful treatment of inflation in the Soviet Union may be shaped more by political and cultural traditions unique to the USSR than by economics as such. Similarly, cultural differences in such crucial dimensions as child-bearing and the induction of adolescents into adulthood clearly have profound implications for educational philosophers and practitioners.

Two centuries ago most Americans lived in small villages and on farms. Today, over two-thirds of the American people reside in metropolitan areas and depend for their incomes not on agriculture but on industry and commerce. This shift in life conditions has implications for how people behave, and what they expect (and get) from government. These changes in the subjects studied by social scientists significantly complicate the conduct and restrict the utility of social science for school administrators.

Administration can be an exciting occupation partly because there are very few "automatics"; each problem and decision is somewhat different from any other. No doubt the apparent unpredictability of administrative phenomena lends zest to the sense of achievement (perhaps mixed with a dose of masochism) that seems to characterize many successful administrators.

Having paid homage at the altar of anomaly, however, I must also suggest that there *are* orderly relationships, discovered and yet to be discovered, in the universe of administrative phenomena. The social and behavioral sciences offer a wealth of theories and tools of analysis that will assist administrators to reduce the uncertainties in decision-making. There are ways of thinking about decision-making which hold promise of greatly improving the probability that a given decision will accomplish what the decision-maker intends to accomplish. This approach suggests that theory and practice are conceptually, and actually, inseparable, and that the concept of hypothesis (and hypothesis testing) should be more closely connected to decision-making by educational administrators.

The Hypothesis

The great English scientist, Thomas Henry Huxley, once wrote that "science is nothing but trained and organized common sense." If that is so the intellectual center of science must surely be the hypothesis, or a statement that explains and predicts events much more accurately than could be done by chance alone. Unfortunately many educational administrators, perhaps most, believe that hypotheses, and the theories on which they are based, are isolated in the laboratory, research journal, or professor's brain; they see no relevance of theory to the world in which they work. This attitude has been reinforced by many graduate training programs in educational administration, which have frequently suffered by admitting students with less than rigorous undergraduate liberal educations and failing to immerse the fledgling administrator in the study of such empirical literature about administration as is available. It is fair to say that most educational administrators do not understand the practical ways that methods of scientific inquiry can aid them in solving the practical problems they face.

Theory and practice are inherently interrelated, because theories are in part induced from the world of everyday events and are statements that explain the relationships among events, and also because intelligent "practice" always involves the process of hypothesizing, even though that process may be unconscious.

Hypotheses thus represent the intellectual cement which binds together theory and practice. Hypotheses are the operationalized expressions of theories, and theories are used in rationales to support the plausibility of specific hypotheses. Decisions can be thought of as hypotheses requiring some reasonable basis for believing that the consequences of the decision are accurately anticipated at the time the decision is made. The basis for such belief lies primarily in the realm of previously tested theory, in statements about before-after and cause-effect relationships. The deliberate use of theory to shape rationales for decisions increases the chances that a decision's consequences can be correctly predicted.

This process of reasoning requires the thoughtful decision-maker to compare as carefully as possible the actual consequences of the decision with the consequences originally predicted before the decision was made. This *testing* of decisions is logically analogous to the hypothesis-testing of the social scientist; differences in the two processes have mainly to do with the scientist's ability to control experimentally or statistically for effects of variables extraneous to the decision (hypothesis), controls that are frequently impractical for the practicing decision-maker to employ. But the thinking process, the critical review of predicted and actual effects of decisions and hypotheses, is identical in both cases and is at the heart of the constant reexamination of doctrine that distinguishes the adapting, improving profession from the uncritical profession choking on the deduced truths of its own unexamined traditions.

Educational decision-makers no longer are allowed the luxury of being only managers/administrators concerned solely or even primarily with faithful trusteeship of an institution while ignoring society's deepest dilemmas. The contemporary educational decision-maker finds his problems inseparably enmeshed with the traumatic racial, religious, social, and economic issues that divide American society. The decision-maker must understand the historical and philosophical backgrounds of the issues he confronts, and apply that understanding to practical fiscal, personnel, and instructional decisions within the context of the organizational structure in which schools are governed, and the societal context in which they function. In making wise decisions the skillful educational leader integrates facts and judgment about the legal structure of education, the broad societal context, and specific areas in which decisions must be made, as well as the overall public policy implications of educational decisions. Disciplined and systematic thinking of Herculean proportions is required; dogged devotion to tradition, to professional dogma, or to an archaic and unproductive insistence that "theory" and "practice" are somehow separate domains is a dangerous denial of the opportunity to think hypothetically and creatively about the real problems facing educational institutions in America today.

Law

Since *Brown v Board of Education of Topeka* in 1954, court decisions have profoundly affected education. I refer to decisions on reapportionment and separation between church and state, as well as to the subsequent desegregation cases. Courts make education policy when they function to define and mediate the impact that fundamental religious, racial, and economic cleavages have on schools. Most recently, the *Serrano* family of school finance cases opens to judicial review many aspects of both taxation and schooling as well as school finance. Courts are now being asked to examine issues of teacher selection and promotion, sex discrimination, and the constitutional rights of students. However, the importance of the judicial process in educational policy-making goes largely unnoticed in major schools of education, which almost without exception lack first-class legal scholarship in their instructional and research programs. University programs for the preparation of educational administrators concentrate almost exclusively on administrative politics, occasionally on legislative politics, but almost never on the crucial role played by courts in the determination of educational policies. Training programs in educational administration must pay increased attention to the changing role of law in public education.

Political Philosophy

I have attached the label of "political philosophy" to the second dimension of thought, which some of us intend to connect more directly to educational administration theory and practice. It is now well over one hundred years since that great evangelist, Horace Mann, popularized his concept of how to institutionalize our unique experiment in mass education. We now find ourselves with a compulsory tax-supported public education system of which Mann would be proud, but which displays dangerous signs of rigidity and ossification. In most states, each child is required to attend a specific school, to sit in a particular seat in an assigned classroom under the control of an assigned teacher. For most children the school controls what subjects the child will study, and even the precise time to be devoted to each subject. Schools classify children by age, race, "intelligence," sex, and by emotional and physical characteristics. Although such classifications may have profound consequences throughout the life of the child, classification practices are frequently based on ambiguous and subjective criteria and allow virtually no procedural safeguards or means of appeal. How many school administrators or professors of educational administration have seriously thought about the judicial doctrine of "due process" in terms of school children? In this sense, American schools are authoritarian institutions operating under a cloak of democratic and participatory rhetoric.

Need education be so rigidly structured? Are there clear and acceptable rationales justifying such arbitrary practices? Is the knowledge base of education sufficiently reliable that it is reasonable to vest such power in presumably expert professionals?

There are people thinking through bits and pieces of these questions. Some press for teacher and administrator accountability. Some sue to gain parental access to previously secret school records. Others propose "alternative" curricula, and still others seek voucher plans allowing parental choice in selecting which school a child will attend. Widespread public skepticism exists about the desirability and effectiveness of present arrangements. To help understand this process, we must rethink the connections between *social function* and *institutional mechanisms*.

The time has come for a basic reexamination of the monopolistic and coercive aspects of public education. Such a basic reexamination raises questions which lie behind such currently visible issues as accountability and economic trends. The questions may be on the distant horizon of today's concerns but will claim increasing attention in the next decade. Fundamental questions must be raised about the structure and function of educational enterprises in this society. I offer four to be considered.

1. Should government compel children to acquire an education? What are the social, political, and economic rationales for compulsoriness? What are the psychological consequences to such mass coercion? Are nineteenth century arguments about the social integration function of schools equally valid to a society with few immigrants, a mobile population, limited bilingual problems, and television? And if government should be empowered to compel the acquisition of education, can twelve years of compulsoriness be justified? Is one latent function of compulsory education to compel belief in a common system of social values (e.g., acceptance of a corporate, bureaucratized society in which social class and income differences are to be accepted as givens)? If this is so, what does the First Amendment's guarantee of freedom of belief really mean? (Note that even if one answers these questions affirmatively one has not necessarily taken a position regarding governmental financing or provision of education.)

2. Should government finance the acquisition of education? If so, is there really a compelling rationale for allowing one public monopoly to be the only publically financed means of becoming educated? (A decision to finance education need not mean that government must also provide educational services.)

3. Should government provide educational services? Should government provide only one or a variety of means for acquiring educa-

tion? Family, TV and cable TV, books, self, profit-making corpo-
rations, and travel offer other means. Should government-financing
mechanisms stimulate choice or reinforce coercion? (Note that an affirmative position here need not lead one to the conclusion that government should discourage nonpublic education by withholding
financial support.)

4. Even if the answers to the preceding questions are all affirmative, must schools be quite so authoritarian and provide so little opportunity for exercise of parental and pupil preferences?

In raising these questions I suggest no answers. I am neither indirectly nor coyly joining any particular camp of reformers. But I do
argue that it is both timely and desirable that first premises of the
political philosophy of education be brought out of the murky back
recesses of our thinking; that the value dimensions of educational
structure, financing, and operation be vigorously analyzed and debated; that educators reexamine why schools in a democratic society
provide virtually no choice to parents and pupils; and finally, that
those who profess to study and practice educational administration
insist on the inclusion of political philosophical perspectives as an
honored component in educational administration. Such questions
may be more likely to be analyzed and debated during periods of
rapid change in enrollments and revenues than during more tranquil
periods of relative equilibrium.

9. Advice from the Field

As a further check on perceptions about the changing role of educational administration and altered loads of preparing them, the ideas of four individuals long experienced in educational matters are presented here. Reflected in these ideas are the experiences of a veteran public junior college administrator, a public school superintendent, a university administrator and critic of higher education, and a statesman of education whose career has placed him at the center of virtually every educational movement since the 1920s.*

In recent years the task of educational administrators has become infinitely more complicated than it was, say, at the end of World War II. In earlier times administrators were expected to lead and to make decisions, and to an appreciable extent they did. However, such prerogative has come to be limited by (1) the increasing protection accorded to the rights and views of individuals and (2) the privileges claimed by the many different constituencies with which an educational institution must relate. The educational administrator must

*This chapter is based on remarks made by John Dunn, William Cunningham, Ralph W. Tyler, and Frank Newman.

consult with many different individuals and groups before reaching decisions. If such diverse constituencies offered generally harmonious and similar advice, the task of administration would be relatively easy. However, the views of the pluralistic society are typically refracted in the advice given the educational leader and his task often becomes one of mediating between conflicting attitudes, points of view, and postures. The problem is most clearly exemplified by the rise of unionism, collective bargaining, and the negotiated contract. Such developments have generally resulted in a transfer of power from its traditional locus into new agencies and instrumentalities which must be consulted before even the smallest decision can be reached. Collective bargaining has changed radically one of the more important tasks of administration, which is dealing with personnel.

Learning to operate in this more constrained context requires substantially different kinds of academic preparation for administration. First, it appears essential that the school administrator should be a practicing psychologist, prepared for that role through work in psychology that calls for dealing intelligently with various points of view. The administrator must be adept at communication, especially in identifying who is listening so that the message can be appropriately phrased. Appropriate phrasing means that the use of the technical idiom must be minimized or eliminated, because most of those with whom administrators must communicate are not technically trained.

The educational administrator must also be a sociologist, attuned to the social configurations of many different groups in a society, including groups not before directly affected by the educational enterprise. As education approaches the steady state it will be expected to extend itself into new areas in response to new needs that must be correctly and accurately gauged. For example, it seems likely that there will be a substantial expansion of off-campus programs, which must be conducted quite differently from on-campus programs, with the campus community relatively tightly controlled. In addition the educational leader should be exposed to work in political science, for he must be a skilled politician, alert to existing and emerging political trends. Much of his work must be done with local political groups, state legislatures, and, of course, the various national political bureaucracies.

The study of psychology, sociology, and political science should be required to develop sensitivity, but other academically produced skills are essential. The administrator must clearly understand public finance and the economic principles on which it rests. He must have some understanding of the law and the ability to identify and use competent legal advice. Obviously he needs to know in detail such important documents as the state education code. However, it should be stressed that he probably does not need the sort of preparation provided by programs in management for the private sector, which can use as a criterion of effectiveness a profit-and-loss statement. Were education administrators to use strictly an economic criterion, the educational steady state would produce a bleak landscape indeed.

With such skills and insights the new administrator should be able to move with some degree of comfort into an emerging new role, one which stresses persuasion and requires mediation rather than the earlier individually determined decisiveness.

The clusters of characteristics and skills required by educational administrators may be quickly summarized. Absolute integrity at all times is essential. Administrators should be open, keeping nothing secret with the possible exception of personnel records. Especially desirable is the willingness and ability to admit error. Sensitivity to others and to situations is of the same order as is willingness to share credit, to share authority, to share ideas, and to share happiness over successes with others involved in the same enterprise. The ideal administrator should like people, for a leadership essential is dealing with people. A sense of humor, or even a sense of the absurd, is necessary to provide the perspective necessary to avoid taking oneself too seriously. The educational leader should have the ability to listen and should especially be master of techniques to ensure that listening has been accurate. Because educational institutions intersect with so many different constituencies and kinds of problems, one who would lead an educational institution must have great tolerance for diversity and ambiguity. He should have the ability to articulate, for much of his time is spent in verbal communication seeking to clarify not just reality, but perceptions of reality. He should have a positive and optimistic attitude, which would include self-confidence tempered by the humility that comes from realizing that one really knows only a few things. Since the functioning of complex bureaucracies relies on morale, the leader should be able to inspire loyalty. And since adversity does happen frequently, courage is also an essential ingredient.

These traits are very likely developed long before the administrator enters a training program, hence they probably cannot really be significantly affected by an educational program. However, there are a number of skills that seem amenable to the influence of education. Quickly summarized, these are: (1) the ability to coordinate the efforts of complex and changing groups of people and of individuals; (2) the ability to identify, analyze, and manage crises; (3) the ability to solve complex problems; (4) the ability to manage time so that the myriad demands can be met without frenzy; (5) the ability to understand and use legal techniques, legal reasoning, and legal information; (6) the ability to deal with budgets and other financial documents; (7) an understanding of the nature of learning so that the essential purposes of an educational institution can be achieved; and (8) awareness of various systems of management available and the ability to select the most appropriate.

Such skills are probably best developed in actual administrative work experience. Thus a training program for future administrators might well require a two-year internship providing a variety of work experience. If at all possible, every candidate for a degree should be provided some experience in government and some hands-on experience in the processes of mediation. Because the applied seems so essential, future administrators should be largely taught by practitioners or those who have had quite recent practical experience. And because educational practices change so rapidly, educational institutions should develop programs for concentrated retraining efforts for practitioners, to take place every two or three years. And because the essential purpose of educational experience and educational institutions is teaching and learning, administrators, especially principals, should be required to meet classes as a teacher every three or four years.

A complex society cannot survive without a major educational industry. Homes, churches, or other social institutions are inadequate to teach the young person all the things he needs to know to function effectively in American society. Romantics may call for de-schooling, but de-schooling can only work in a primitive society. Even though education may be approaching a steady state, there should be no dearth of exciting educational problems to solve. The depression decade of the 1930s presented education with all the principal attributes of a steady or declining state industry. Enrollments were low, especially in the elementary schools, faculty salaries were cut seriously, and institutional budgets were frequently cut 50 percent or more. Yet from the standpoint of education, the period of the 1930s was one of the most creative periods in the history of American education. Psychometrics as a technique began to bloom, new kinds of vocational programs were developed, and general education as a major force emerged.

The anticipated steady state of the 1970s and eighties presents a number of challenging problems that education must solve. One of these is to devise ways of teaching large numbers of students who were previously of little concern to education. An analogy may be drawn with the practice of medicine: When adequate medical service was available only to the middle and upper classes, medical practice was relatively straightforward. An offending organism or organ simply had to be removed or neutralized and the basic health of the middle-class individual would reestablish itself. Once medical service was extended to groups of people who had not had an adequate diet, who had not been trained to take good care of themselves physically, new techniques of providing medical service had to be developed, ranging from motivating a patient to take needed medicine regularly to rectifying the effects of long years of dietary deficiency. Similarly, as long as education dealt with the children of the middle and upper classes, processes were relatively straightforward. Children already had been taught a desire to learn, to defer gratification, and to expect success. As education is extended to other segments of the population, those attributes are not always to be found. Education must devise new ways of motivating, new ways of presenting information, and new ways of gauging success.

Another problem is to find new ways of inducting the young into adult society, now that many once-operative techniques are no longer sufficiently potent. As the quest goes on, such techniques may include much more pre-school education and after-school education as essential devices of socialization.

A third problem is to devise new methods for providing comprehensive occupational education. In previous times schools succeeded relatively well in preparing students who would go on to college and for a few very technical vocations. But schools failed for some 35 to 50 percent of the students, simply because their talents and interests did not mesh with existing society. Schooling was, in a very real sense, a screening device that screened out of the mainstream of

American life those who did not conform. By 1970, however, virtually all major segments of the population will require schooling, especially for vocations, and ways must be found to ensure the relevance of that education as well as its adaptability to new kinds of students.

Another problem is to define the school's role in character development. The general need for character education is accepted, but as the influence of the home and church on character has declined schools have not fully faced up to their responsibility in this area.

As education seeks to deal with such problems, the role of administration becomes more important. The overarching postulate is that education is more important in the 1970s than in the past because society is more complex and education has a wider range of problems to solve. Administrators are expected to give leadership to schools as they try to solve those problems. Unless administrators understand the underlying problems of education, they either become impotent leaders or followers of fads. Many educational fads can be of value, but they become woven into long-lasting educational fabric only if the underlying problems they seek to solve are thoroughly understood. If administrators take the time to think deeply about these problems, the 1970s could conceivably be as exciting as were the 1930s.

While in some respects higher education and lower education are quite distinct from each other, they each must face several broad questions that stem from a steady state.

The first question has to do with the structure of education and educational institutions, which can encourage appropriate competition and at the same time discourage inappropriate and destructive competition, especially in the political sphere. Unless those in charge of education are watchful, the competition for scarce resources implied by a steady state will produce self-defeating political manipulation as various organizational entities compete for influence or for funds. The much-discussed push for public accountability could lead more to public relations efforts than to actual educational reforms. Education has generally responded to demands for public accountability and formulas to bring about standardized cost with defensiveness or reluctant provision of requested data. A better course would be to avoid the attempt to standardize costs and to create a situation in which educational competition expressed through the marketplace is the technique used for controlling institutions. The marketplace concept has apparently produced useful research. If an appropriate structure were developed, that same sort of marketplace could produce more effective education.

A second question relates to the functions or purposes of collegiate institutions. In the past, colleges were able to maintain a balance between their efforts to prepare people for careers and to prepare people for life. This was possible because a small number of young people attended college and there were enough spaces in the middle- and upper-middle-class vocations to absorb them. By the 1970s that balance had been destroyed. Institutions that concentrate on preparation for the vocations find that there are no places for their graduates to go, yet much of the motivation bringing new kinds of students to college stems from vocational needs. What colleges and universities must do is separate preparation for jobs from preparation for life, and make clear to prospective students that going through a given educational program may or may not have vocational relevance. This means that institutions and the entire society must downgrade credentialing, while at the same time they develop programs to ensure a great deal of personal and vocational flexibility. This very likely will require that the traditional ordering of kinds of educational experiences be altered. Previously it was assumed that the young person received liberalizing education first and then vocational education, after which all formal educational activity ceased.

A third issue has to do with reversing the trend for education to give way in favor of schooling. At one time collegiate education stressed education in a broad sense, with many campus elements contributing to it. However, by the 1950s the stage had narrowed to classrooms, simple transmission of information, and gaining credentials. Colleges had become very good at providing schooling, but quite ineffective at educating people.

These are complex problems, not at all easy to solve. However, several suggestions can be advanced.

1. Greater attention must be given to institutional structure that will produce ways by which competition can be used to achieve educational ends.

2. The rewards for teaching must be changed. One reason why traditional modes of teaching persevere is that they require little effort. Almost every innovation or reform in teaching requires addi-

tional effort, which will only be expended if the reward structure is modified.

3. The traditional ordering of curricular elements must be drastically altered, so that liberalizing, character building, or vocational education is received at various periods during an individual's lifetime.

4. Professionals involved in higher education rarely take the time to discuss the processes of their profession. This must be changed if the problems of a steady state are to be confronted.

10. Postscript

The rationale and program for the preparation of educational administrators described in this book is bound to produce varying reactions. While many reactions will be positive and approving of the general kinds of changes suggested, others, quite understandably, will be negative and critical of parts or all of the planned program. Such reactions are deserving of serious response.

Some practicing school administrators, particularly those prepared for the most part by professors who themselves had been successful school administrators, find it difficult to conceive of an effective administration faculty composed largely of individuals who do not have substantial administrative experience. To them administration is viewed more as an art best cultivated in a quasi-apprenticeship situation, in which those who have trod the path earlier point the way for the aspirant. Related is the fact of alumni loyalty. Alumni of collegiate and professional institutions represent one of the strongest buttresses for the American system of higher education. However, alumni frequently tend to idealize the experiences they themselves had and hence find it difficult to accept change, especially such a profound change as altering the essential composition of a faculty. Also related is the demonstrable fact of differences in life-style, language, and even temperament, of those individuals attracted to the professoriate and those attracted to the practice of administration. There is nothing invidious in these differences, but they can make communication and mutual understanding somewhat difficult. To the practicing administrator, the professor (particularly one without administrative experience) may appear overly concerned with theory, unable to reach unqualified decisions and preoccupied and intrigued with complexity for its own sake. The professor may regard the decisions of administrators as overly simplistic and discourse about administration more homiletic than illuminating. This phenomenon probably operates in all academic settings, but is likely more intensely revealed in prestigious institutions.

Different but equally skeptical reactions are manifested by other constituencies. Specialized groups of graduate students, such as those enrolled in the study of higher educational administration, express fear that a common core of experiences for aspiring administrators for all levels will somehow destroy a desirable discreteness. This is particularly revealed in the fear that reemphasizing the Ed.D. degree will place them at a disadvantage. They are struck with the apparent prestige of the Ph.D. degree in American higher education, and feel that without such a degree their opportunities for high positions of leadership would be seriously restricted. There are also those who are concerned about the assumption of a steady state in American education when there are large segments of the population who need more education and who, if served, could absorb the creative energies of increasing numbers of professionals. To them, programs that will restrict the number of students and graduates is tantamount to denial of an enormous social responsibility. Such individuals are somewhat resentful of the elitist connotations of a restricted program, believing that the real educational need is for many thousands of new educational workers to cope with new and expanding problems rather than for a few attempting to exert leadership at a high level. A third separate group could be categorized as academic purists who believe that becoming involved in practice and application dilutes the essential nature of university scholarship. They tend to believe that university professors are true to their calling only when preoccupied with their discipline at a high level of abstraction. Because the American Ph.D. degree has gained worldwide respect as reflecting a pure version of scholarship, such individuals are likely to resent applied doctoral degrees as debasing that respect.

And, of course, there are quite understandable and human idiosyncratic reactions that must be understood and accommodated. When practitioners of administration are asked for advice and they give it, their resentment is understandable if the advice is not taken. Some have felt that an academic program could be conceived of as an abstraction, not to be particularly dependent on the tastes and interests of specific faculty members; to them, a program built around idiosyncratic talents and interests of a faculty is suspect. Then too, individual expectations of such things as faculty appointments play a role. The announcement of a new position in administration at Alma Mater does lead to expectations on the part of distinguished graduates that they would likely be the most appropriate candidate. If a different sort of appointment is made, some very human resentment can be generated.

It is not only external constituencies that have misgivings about a program for the preparation of educational administrators. The involved faculty members may also be worried and skeptical. Some of their perplexities can be quickly summarized, and are in many respects parallel to the uneasiness of constituencies. Can a faculty predominantly composed of research scholars really provide the kind of preparation and training that will produce successful administrators? The assumption here is that this is indeed possible, but the worry persists.

It appears increasingly obvious that retraining and continuing education of administrators in the field is not only desirable but essential. However, this raises the question whether the time of a faculty heavily committed to research and scholarship can readily be redeployed to provide service to the field. For example, can a viable summer school and in-service training program be developed and implemented by faculty members accustomed to using summer time to pursue individual research interests? The answer to this and similar questions rests on the answer to an even broader question: Can field-oriented professors and programs be maintained comfortably and successfully in a university in which the major pressures and statuses are associated with research and scholarship? This matter becomes particularly pointed when a school attempts to appoint a professor who can satisfy expectations of active practitioners and at the same time satisfy the scholarly expectations of a university faculty.

Other, more mundane, worries also intrude. The easy availability of external student support is a thing of the past. Can a high-cost, largely residential program attract needed numbers of students in the absence of substantial amounts of student scholarship and fellowship support? Will aspiring educational administrators opt for a high-cost institution when there are relatively low-cost public institutions that offer training and credentialing for comparable positions? The other side of this coin, of course, is whether a privately controlled and supported university can maintain high-quality programs for relatively small numbers of students. Tuition is an essential fact of life for all save two or three graduate programs in education. Small numbers of students, with the attendant small amounts of tuition payment, means that an adequate faculty must probably be supported out of unrestricted university funds. The question is then how much support a university is willing to provide.

A few other worries can complete this litany. Students attracted to the study of education have typically not been particularly accomplished in quantitative skills; can such students be brought to the level of quantitative sophistication deemed necessary for the preparation of administrators for the future? Can the interests of a research-oriented faculty be sustained in a program for the training of practitioners when their own research interests are likely to shift to conform to the evolution of the various research disciplines?

These are all serious concerns, and most of them have been responded to earlier in this book. However, it seems desirable to make a response in the form of a credo to which a faculty in educational administration can subscribe.

1. We believe that the various practices in education are professional activities of a high order which require sophisticated, intellectual training. We also believe that educational administration is a high and desirable calling and that many of the professional skills needed can be developed or inculcated.

2. We believe that the university is the most appropriate place for the fundamental preparation and training of administrators. While we value highly applied experience and apprenticeship kinds of learning, we also believe that the university, with its stress on conceptual learning and theory, should provide the base on which experiential learning takes place.

3. We accept the fact of a distinctiveness that separates the academic from the applied, but believe that this need not be invidious nor destructive. Academics and practicing administrators function in different contexts and employ different techniques. Properly understood, however, these differences can be mutually supportive, which leads us to the belief that

4. Scholarship and practicality are not only not incompatible, but are mutually beneficial. Scholarship without contact with reality becomes sterile, just as practice without scholarship becomes shallow and superficial.

5. We believe in the continuity of social institutions and, in this context, educational institutions. We also believe that change in strategy or in technique is the rule. We have advanced a particular rationale for a program in educational administration, fully realizing that modifications are inevitable and that at a different time, under different circumstances, a different rationale and strategy would probably have been suggested.

6. We believe in the concept of a socially responsible elite whose talents and training equip them to exert significant influence over the course of human events. We also believe that such elites properly can be prepared in educational institutions which accept that responsibility, while at the same time they reject other equally worthy missions.

7. We do not believe that a university is able to develop or even cultivate *all* the traits, skills, and attributes needed by educational leaders. Many characteristics, such as courage, integrity, self-confidence, or humility, evolve from childhood over a lifetime, and there is little that a formal advanced educational program can do to affect them. Traits such as sensitivity to an individual's conditions or problems are probably cultivated best in many different situations, and are probably affected only slightly through formal course work, research, or conceptualizing. A university should be parsimonious in what it claims to do, but should seek to do extraordinarily well those things for which it is best equipped.

8. We believe that many of the differences that arise between different constituencies can in large measure be resolved through continuous dialogue. Thus, within the university the differences between adherents to different academic disciplines can be resolved through

sustained dialogue, just as conversations between the academic and the practical can bring the two efforts into harmony.

9. Lastly, we believe that while this report is largely concerned with the School of Education at Stanford University, much of what has been said is generalizable to other institutions.

APPENDIX

Programs in Administration and Policy Analysis: Guidelines for Students

General Introduction to the Stanford Program

General Objectives

The Stanford Program in Educational Administration seeks to produce leaders, those who will shape the future nature of educational organizations and those who will be thoughtful and resourceful research scholars.

The Program prepares administrators and scholars distinguished by their understanding of societal forces and of complex organizations, and by their ability to question, analyze, and develop creative answers to policy and operating problems and make decisions even though conflict and ambiguity exist. It is characterized by its intellectual approach and its base in the behavioral sciences. It is built around a core of conceptual and quantitative understanding, knowledge, and analytical skills applied to the internal and external environment and the functions and technologies of administration.

Within the total Program there is a high degree of flexibility, with options consonant with the student's career plans. Individual plans vary as to degree level (master's, doctorate), institutional focus (higher education, public or private elementary and secondary schools, state or federal organizations), and arena (administration, research). The resources of the entire University are available, and students are encouraged to take advantage of the competencies of Stanford's outstanding faculties. In addition to their classwork, students test their knowledge and values in significant field situations.

The faculty for the Program in Administration and Policy Analysis is an unusual one. Most members have been trained in one of the several relevant social or behavioral sciences. All are deeply involved in ongoing research and scholarship; all are also directly concerned with actual practices of administration. The faculty is almost evenly divided between professors who have had extensive administrative experience at various levels of education, and those who have made the theory and practice of Administration and Policy Analysis the focus of their major scholarly endeavors. Such a faculty provides students opportunities for rigorous disciplinary study, for interdisciplinary study, and for creative application of knowledge to administration.

A university is a house of intellect, and students entering the Program must be intellectually able. What is sought in prospective students is high intelligence and a record of past experience indicating motivation, perseverance, and leadership potential. Students are welcomed if they desire to join a community of scholars in a rigorous and demanding program. Although many students acquire a credential in connection with their work at Stanford, and a few may, through force of circumstances, do some part-time work in the Program, neither is quest for the credential the primary purpose of the Program, nor part-time study the usual mode. The normal student will pursue one of three distinctive degree programs and will be expected to devote full time to the Program.

Special Subdivisions

The Program in Administration and Policy Analysis is intended to facilitate interaction among students having many different career goals. Thus a spirit of collegiality is fostered. However, the Program does allow for several different emphases. When applying, students may wish to specify the emphasis in which they are interested but should also realize the likelihood of changing goals as a result of their experiences at Stanford.

1. *Elementary and Secondary Administration*

For those who plan to take administrative, analytical, or research positions in the public schools, state and federal agencies, foundations, and research laboratories, in management or central administrative positions. Students should possess strong aptitudes both in analyzing problems and in quantitative applications. Some particular areas of focus are taxation, educational expenditures, intergovernmental aid, program planning, budgeting systems, cost-benefit and cost-effectiveness analysis, the return from educational investment, organizational design, and managerial decision-making, supervision of instruction, curricular supervision, supervision of personnel.

2. *Higher Education Administration*

The concentration in higher education is intended to prepare people to enter administrative posts in higher education, for the most part concerned with central and academic administration but not excluding student personnel work or financial administration. Some students may also use the program as preparation for teaching and research concerning higher education as an area of study. The program is designed to be flexible so that students through elective courses and dissertation work may, if they wish to, concentrate on any of a number of subspecialties in higher education (curriculum, institutional research, planning, admissions, or development). Stanford does not have a program directed exclusively to the preparation of junior college administrators. However, the doctoral program at Stanford does qualify candidates for roles in junior colleges. The peculiar problems of junior colleges are generally considered and discussed in the general context of American higher education.

3. *Policy Analysis*

For those who plan to take positions in local, regional, state, national, or international agencies and organizations and who plan to work with policy considerations and issues. Various emphases are possible, including politics, economics, finance, or long-range goal setting and planning for complex systems of education. Increasingly American education is a complex enterprise requiring sophisticated policy formation and implementation. It is to prepare people to deal with those complexities and issues that this emphasis is designed.

4. *Joint Education/Business School Program*

In this program the student simultaneously pursues a master's degree in business administration (a Business School degree) and a doctorate in education. The purposes of the program are: (1) to provide an administrative core drawing on the resources of the Graduate School of Business and Graduate School of Education (course work takes up subjects from the viewpoint of the practicing manager); (2) to include in the doctoral phase significant stress on curriculum design and the learning process; (3) to attract new people to education, some of whom indicated an initial interest in the general management training provided by GSB. GSB courses such as microeconomics, management and the computer, operations and systems analysis, organizational behavior, business finance, and operations management, include general concepts and analytical skills that are applicable to education. The School of Education Administration and Policy Analysis faculty will provide course work in such areas as school finance, economics of education, and education and public policy. Applicants apply to and enroll initially in the Graduate School of Business, but they are also assigned an adviser in the School of Education. It is expected that most Joint Program students will elect to complete the Urban Management Option in the MBA program in the Graduate School of Business. After completion of the MBA program, students apply to transfer to the School of Education to complete the requirements for the Ph.D. or Ed.D. degree in Education. Course work taken in the School of Business will transfer to satisfy some of the School of Education requirements. Some elective courses for the MBA may be fulfilled by completing courses in the School of Education.

Programs and Degrees

The Administration and Policy Analysis Committee of the School of Education offers its programs to culminate in one of three different degrees, depending on the career objectives of students.

1. *The Master's Degree*

The degree of Master of Arts in Education with specialization in Administration and Policy Analysis is a one-year program designed for individuals who will be working as the consultants and staff officers in state or federal educational agencies, in specialized administrative positions, in colleges and universities or school districts, for which some work beyond the bachelor's degree is appropriate. The master's program consists of approximately 75 percent prescribed work taken by all students in the programs offered and the remaining 25 percent electives, according to each student's professional interests or aspirations. Prospective students may apply for the master's degree program and all students who successfully complete the first full academic year will be awarded the degree of Master of Arts in Education with a concentration in Administration and Policy Analysis.

2. *The Ed.D. Degree*

The Ed.D. degree is designed to prepare individuals, through development of sophisticated management skills, for a wide variety of educational leadership positions in many different levels of education. It is equally applicable for individuals aspiring to school superintendencies and administrative positions in junior and four-year colleges and universities, or to individuals wishing high-level positions in educationally related organizations and agencies. It is expected that the large majority of students completing a doctoral degree in Administration and Policy Analysis at Stanford will receive the Ed.D. degree. The program will include completion of a set of core course requirements, additional work in professional education, a minimum of 12 units of work outside the School of Education, a supervised internship, and a thesis or a dissertation usually of an applied nature. The program will normally require three to four years beyond receipt of the bachelor's degree, or between two and three years beyond receipt of a master's degree. While the program of any given individual will vary according to his or her needs and interests, a typical pattern would be four or five quarters of full-time academic course work, two quarters of half-time course work, and internship followed by from two to four quarters' work on a thesis or dissertation.

The Ed.D. dissertation or thesis emphasizes theoretical applications to specific administrative situations or the theoretical interpretation and analysis of the implementation of administrative practice or projects. For example, the faculty and a student could arrange with a local school district or college to implement a specific educational program or new administrative role. Students in the policy analysis emphasis could evaluate alternative federal or state programs in such areas as finance, child care, or college scholarships. The dissertation might be a critical analysis of the administration of a project with considerable stress on the relationship of theoretical concepts to operating situations.

3. *The Ph.D. Degree*

The Ph.D. degree in Administration and Policy Analysis is a research degree and is intended for those who aspire to become professors of administration or to devote themselves principally to research and scholarship concerning educational institutions and their organization and administration. The program emphasizes preparation for making contributions to the fundamentals underlying educational administration, and draws heavily on such academic disciplines as history, sociology, political science, psychology, economics, or some coherent interdisciplinary combination of those fields. For example, a Ph.D. recipient might specialize in operations analysis applied to education, in organizational behavior in educational institutions, or in the process of educational policy formation.

Each graduate must complete the basic core program required of all students in Administration and Policy Analysis. In addition, each must demonstrate a high level of professional competence in four broad areas:

• *A substantial field of scholarly study relevant to educational administration.* The field may consist in a recognized academic discipline (e.g., economics, sociology, history); it may be a well-defined and coherent interdisciplinary field. In either case, the expectation is that the candidate will have the knowledge equivalent to one full year of graduate study in the research training programs of the appropriate department, departments, or schools at Stanford.

• *The methodology of research.* The research training required is that defined as appropriate for doctoral students in the field of study in which the candidate claims competence.

• *Statistics.* The minimum statistical competence is that provided by Education 250A, B, C. Most candidates are required, because of the nature of their fields of study, to secure additional training in advanced statistics, multivariate techniques, and mathematical models.

• *The institutional context of educational administration.* Each candidate must demonstrate a scholarly awareness of the legal, social, political, organizational, and economic context of higher education, precollegiate education, or educational policy-making in government agencies.

4. *General Degree Considerations*

Generally a student is encouraged to defer until the latter part of the first year the decision whether the master's degree, the Ed.D., or the Ph.D. will best meet his professional needs. At that time the student and his adviser will reach a decision and outline a full program in one of the emphases offered.

A normal academic course load in the School of Education is four courses of approximately four units each per term. The minimum requirement for a doctoral degree is 108 units beyond the bachelor's degree. It is estimated that a typical person holding a relevant master's degree will require approximately 85 units, including thesis and internship credit for an Ed.D. degree. A typical Ph.D. candidate who has a relevant disciplinary master's degree will require approximately 91 units, including the dissertation. A student with only a bachelor's degree or with a master's degree not clearly relevant to the Program should anticipate a program with at least 108 units of work.

5. *Administrative Credential Program*

Stanford's program can meet the administrative or supervisory credential requirements for California and many other states. Students desiring credentials for some particular state should discuss this with their adviser immediately on arrival at Stanford in order better to plan appropriate programs.

Elements of the Programs in Administration and Policy Analysis

Master's Degree in Administration and Policy Analysis

A minimum of 48 units of graduate work is required, of which 36 will be the required core of nine courses required of all students in the programs offered by the Committee on Administration and Policy Analysis.

Doctoral Programs

Stanford offers both the Ph.D. and the Ed.D. degrees. There is substantial difference in content, time, and approach between the two degrees. The following elements are included in one or the other of the two doctoral programs, or both:

1. *Courses*

A minimum of 108 quarter hours or units beyond the bachelor's degree is required of all doctoral students, 36 of which will be the required core of three year-long courses taken during the first year in residence. Students with relevant graduate work elsewhere may receive credit for it. However, such credit is not automatic. (Details concerning these courses are described in Core Courses, pp. 178-181, below.)

2. *Courses Outside Education*

The Ph.D. requires approximately 30-36 hours of work in some relevant department or school other than Education. Students make arrangements for such a minor in consultation with their advisers. There is no minor requirement for the Ed.D. degree, but students are nonetheless expected to include much cross-departmental work. A minimum of 12 hours taken outside the School of Education is required.

3. *Internships*

All candidates for the Ed.D. degree in Administration and Policy Analysis will be required to have, or have had, relevant field experience in a working administrative situation. Some students satisfy this requirement through having had appropriate administrative experience prior to attending Stanford. Others acquire this needed experience if their dissertations are clearly done in an administrative context that will expose them to administrative styles and practices. However, the latter are likely to be exceptions, and are subject to receiving approval from the Chairman of the Committee on Administration and Policy Analysis. The general policy is that all students are required to take an internship program of at least two-terms' duration, together with an internship seminar. Internships generally will be taken during the second year in residence, will generally be half-time activities, and will generally be remunerative. Candidates for the Ph.D. degree in Administration and Policy Analysis may also be required to take an internship if, in the opinion of the candidate's adviser, such an experience is essential for the candidate's professional education. Academic credit in the amount of 10 units will be awarded for the internship and seminar.

4. *Values*

Students are expected to consider the various value bases and correlates of educational decisions, and are aided in doing so through exposure to the various value orientations of different faculty members and through taking courses concerned with value questions, e.g., philosophy of education.

5. *Qualifying Procedures*

After admission, students will undergo a series of qualifying procedures culminating in the degree for which the student is working.

• *Master's degree students.* Students accepted into the master's program will not be required to pass any formal qualifying procedures beyond the successful completion of the core courses and at least 12 units of electives. However, master's candidates who, subsequent to matriculation, wish to be considered for admission into one of the two doctoral programs will be expected to apply for consideration and to follow the qualification procedures for candidates in those programs. They will be judged in comparison with new applicants for the doctoral programs.

• *All doctoral students.* The progress of all first-year doctoral students will be reviewed at the end of the second quarter. This review, by the full faculty, will consider class performance and other available data. The purpose of review is to consider the eligibility of students to continue in the doctoral program if they wish to do so.

Early in the fourth quarter of residency Ed.D. candidates will be asked to prepare a paper dealing with an administrative or policy program, specifying an approach to it, and making some preliminary analysis. The purpose of this paper will be to aid the adviser and other faculty members in advising students concerning possible deficiencies in or ways of strengthening the individual's program. This paper and other relevant information will be used at this time as a basis for admission into candidacy. Toward the middle or end of the second year of residency students will be expected to develop a dissertation proposal and to have it approved. Ed.D. candidates are also required to submit to one of three distinct kinds of oral examinations. Option A is a general oral over the student's major field and is normally taken at the end of all course and internship work. Option B is taken at the end of completing a dissertation proposal and is intended to be a defense of that proposal. Option C is a defense of the complete dissertation. Each student should consult with his adviser about the appropriate choice for him.

• *Ph.D. students.* At the end of the second year each Ph.D. student is required to take a qualifying examination demonstrating competence in the areas covered in the first two years of academic work. During the third year, as the candidate prepares a dissertation proposal, he will submit to an oral examination, open to the public, in which he discusses the literature and theory with which his proposal is concerned. A final oral examination in defense of the dissertation is also required.

Student Advisement

Each entering student is assigned to a faculty member as an advisee. This faculty member will help students develop a program for the first several terms. After students become familiar with the faculty they often wish to change advisers to someone whose talents are particularly relevant to the students' interests, and such changes are encouraged. The adviser will help students develop a study program and will generally be available to assist students concerning their educational and career plans, programs, and problems. Because all students will be taking the same core of courses during the first year, considerable group counseling of students is feasible and is done. In addition, students themselves are an important counseling resource. Students organize an area colloquium series that brings distinguished people before the student body, and also assists students in making educational or career decisions.

Admissions Procedures

Acceptance of applicants into the several programs offered by the Committee on Administration and Policy Analysis will be based in large measure on demonstrated academic aptitude, previous academic achievement, and on particularly relevant work experience. Candidates of considerable aptitude and demonstrated academic achievement who have had relevant recent work experiences in one of those three areas may receive some special consideration for those experiences. However, the fact that an individual has had some varied professional experience in education, regardless of how long, does not imply that significant weight will be assigned to that experience. In general, aptitude, as measured by the aptitude tests of the Graduate Record Examination, and achievement, as revealed by grade point averages, will establish the major prerequisites for consideration of experiential factors. The fact that an applicant has indicated a preference for one of the subspecialties will not affect a decision on admission.

The School of Education and Stanford University practice affirmative action in considering various minority group members and women for admission into academic programs. The Committee on Administration and Policy Analysis employs different techniques for gauging aptitude and achievement when standard testing methods appear clearly inappropriate.

The Curriculum

Each doctoral student is expected to have completed a minimum of 108 quarter hours, or units covering nine full quarters of graduate work. Credit up to a total of 36 hours may be given for work done at other institutions, provided the work is of a quality comparable to work at Stanford, is relevant to the individual's program, and is approved by the Chairman of the Committee on Administration and Policy Analysis. Generally graduate academic credit received more than seven years earlier is not acceptable. No more than five units of dissertation credit may be allowed except through approval of the Chairman of the Committee on Administration and Policy Analysis.

There are five kinds of courses for doctoral students in this program: (1) general courses required of all School of Education students; (2) the core courses required of all students in the Administration and Policy Analysis area; (3) specialized courses required in subareas (such as higher education or general administration); (4) Ph.D. minor courses in another department (where applicable); and (5) credits given for internships and dissertation credits. Each of these is examined below.

General School of Education Requirements

In addition to the special courses for this area, the School of Education requires that all doctoral candidates develop advanced competence in what the faculty judges to be four "core" dimensions of professional competence in education, no matter what the particular specialized concentration may be. These four common dimensions, which must be included explicitly in the proposed study program, are:

1. *Studies in Curriculum, Instruction, Administration, and Special Services*

While the courses relevant to this dimension will in most cases be found in the School of Education, use can also be made of relevant cognate studies elsewhere in the University (e.g., law and business organization in the case of doctoral students in school administration).

2. *Behavioral Science Studies*

Behavioral Science studies deal with change, dynamics, and organization in the individual and in society. It is expected that programs will draw on courses outside the School of Education as well as those in the school.

3. *Normative Studies*

Normative studies explore the ideological-historical-philosophical bases for evolving and criticizing policies, aims, and criteria. There are relevant courses in the School of Education and elsewhere in the University for this dimension.

4. *Inquiry Skills*

Inquiry skills studies develop the critical and investigative skills and tools particularly relevant to the area of concentration and to the expected dissertation research. There are relevant courses and seminars in a large number of University departments and schools, as well as in the School of Education.

Core Courses

An essential ingredient of the program in Administration and Policy Analysis is a core of three 3-quarter courses required to be taken during the first year. These are intended to be basic, both to the practice of administration or policy work and to research and scholarship concerning such matters. It is assumed that students will augment this core by taking work in other relevant social sciences, such as psychology or anthropology, which are not explicitly part of the core. The three sequences of courses are indicated below.

> Education ____ , ____ , ____ . 4 credits each. Aut. Win. Spr. *Administration and Organization of Educational Institutions in Context.* An examination of the context within which educational institutions function, the issues they face and how they are organized, governed and administered. One of three required three-term sequences for all programs in *Administration and Policy Analysis* open to other students in Stanford University.
> • Education ____ . *American Educational Institutions* (Hatton). An examination of the context in which educational institutions function, the salient and emerging issues which educational institutions face, and the likely direction of resolution of those issues. A lecture-discus-

sion course, introducing students to different faculty members and requiring students to write intelligently and thoughtfully about each major topic considered.

- Education ____. *Administration and Organization of Post-Secondary Institutions* (Mayhew). An analysis of the nature of postsecondary educational institutions, how they are administered and governed, and tactics and strategies available in the performance of administrative roles.
- Education ____. *Administration and Organization of Public & Private Schools* (Weiner). An analysis of the nature of local educational agencies, schools, and districts; how they are administered and controlled, how leadership is exerted, and the tactics and strategies available to administrators.

Education ____ , ____ , ____ . 4 credits each. Aut. Win. Spr. *Decision Analysis in Education.* A three-quarter sequence in the application of quantitative reasoning and decision-making in education.

- Education ____. *Decision Analysis I* (Faculty). Develops the basic tools for decision-making under uncertainty. The foundation is statistical decision theory. Topics covered include the basics of probability, decision trees and loss tables, sampling and the formation of expectations, the value of information, the statistical decision rules and their error characteristics. A strong background in high school level math or some calculus desirable, but not essential since a math review will be offered in the Autumn term.
- Education ____. *Decision Analysis II* (Faculty). Deals with the problems of measurement, system modeling, and simulation from the point of view of the educational administrator or policy analyst. The focus is on the formation of administrative inference from numbers and the assessment of expert testimony in quantitative form. The course includes an introduction to computers as aids to educational decision-making and to the formation and use of first approximations.
- Education ____. *Decision Analysis III* (Faculty). Con-

siders the problems of optimization and the design and
evaluation of decision experience. Marginal analysis,
cost-benefit accounting, constrained maximization,
mathematical modeling, program evaluation. An introduction to linear models for large-scale data analysis is
provided. Particular attention is paid to the sensitivity
of implications to model assumptions.

Education ___ , ___ , ___ . 4 credits each. Aut. Win. Spr.
The Social Sciences and Educational Analysis. Addresses
itself to the relationships among economics, political science, and sociology and their applications to education.
While the sequence is required of students in the program
on Administration and Policy Analysis, the courses are
open to all students. Although each quarter focuses on the
contribution of a particular social science, an attempt is
made to integrate the subjects by stressing their interrelationships. The courses are taught by appropriate specialists
from each area with some team teaching. The syllabus relies heavily on reading assignments in conjunction with
case studies.

- Education ___ . *Introduction to the Economics of Education* (Levin). An overview of the relationship between
education and economic analysis. Specific attention is
devoted to investment and consumption theories of education and to the financing of education. Particular topics include the effects of education on economic growth
and the distribution of education as well as taxation for
educational purposes. Students who lack training in elementary economics will be required to enroll in a parallel course in economic analysis for one additional unit
of credit.

- Education ___ . *Introduction to the Politics of Education* (Kirst). An overview of the relationship between
political analysis and policy formulation in education.
Specific focus is given to alternative models of the political process, the nature of interest groups, political strategies, community power and the external environment
of organizations, and the implementation of policy. Par-

ticular applications to educational settings and problems
are emphasized.

- Education ____. *Introduction to the Sociology of Education* (Baldridge). An analysis of the links between education and the stratification system in the United States. Topics include: structure of class systems, theories of the origin of class systems, social mobility and education, barriers to educational and social opportunity with a special focus on race and sex, and the recent debates over the meaning and existence of equality of educational opportunity.

Advanced Courses in Administration and Policy Analysis

Other specialized courses are offered by the faculty in Administration and Policy Analysis. The specific number and pattern of these courses to be taken are determined by the student and his adviser. Because all are considered relevant to the entire area of administration and policy analysis, these courses are not segregated as to specific emphasis.

Other Courses within the School of Education

From the wide range of courses students can develop subemphases of particular interest to them, such as supervision of the curriculum or continuing educational innovations. In addition, these courses can rectify deficiencies or gaps which any core set of courses produces.

Courses outside the School of Education

There are many offerings in other schools and departments of significance for students in Administration and Policy Analysis. Especially relevant are courses in the Graduate School of Business, the School of Law, anthropology, communications, economics, engineering, history, political science, sociology, and urban studies.

Examples of Programs

The following tables indicate the general sequence of the Ed.D. and Ph.D. programs. Obviously these must be modified to accommodate the needs, strengths and weaknesses of individual students.

Sequence of Programs: Ed.D. Degree

	Year 1	Year 2	Year 3
Fall	Orientation Core courses Elective courses	Elective courses Quantifying Paper Application for candidacy	Elective courses as needed Preparation of thesis
Winter	Core courses Elective courses Program and progress review	Elective courses Internship Internship seminar Granting of candidacy	Preparation of thesis
Spring	Core courses Elective courses	Elective courses Internship and seminar Preparation of thesis proposal Granting of candidacy	Preparation of thesis and oral examination
Summer	(To be used as needed)		

Sequence of Programs: Ph.D. Degree

	Year 1	Year 2	Year 3	Year 4
Fall	Orientation Core courses Elective courses	Elective educa- tion and disciplinary courses	Elective educa- tion and disciplinary courses	Work on thesis and
Winter	Core courses Elective courses Program and progress review	Elective educa- tion and disciplinary courses Granting of candidacy	Elective and disciplinary courses Public defense of thesis proposal	Oral defense of thesis
Spring	Core courses Elective courses	Elective educa- tion and disciplinary courses	Work on thesis	

Year 1	Year 2	Year 3	Year 4
	Written com-prehension examina-tion		

Summer (To be used as needed)

Samples of Programs for Various Interests

A future school principal who enters with a relevant master's degree:

	Units
Core sequence	36
Education ____ . Schools and Community	4
Education ____ . Leadership in Organization	4
Education ____ . Administration and Organization of Elementary and Secondary Schools	4
Education ____ . Administration and Organization of Complex Systems—Elementary and Secondary Schools	4
Education ____ . School Personnel Policies and Practices	4
Education 205. Philosophies of Education	4
Education 200. History of Education	3
Education 318. Advanced Educational Psychology	4
Education 354. Curriculum Evaluation	4
Education 440. Seminar in the School Curriculum	4
Education ____ . Internship Seminar	10
Thesis	5
	Total 90 beyond the master's degree

A future college admissions director pursuing a master's degree:

	Units
Core sequence	36
Education 255. Human Abilities	3
Education ____ . Technical Problems and Processes in Administration in Higher Education	4

Education ____ . Independent Study on College
Admissions   4

                 Total   47 for a mas-
ter's de-
gree

A future legislative analyst for education working in a state budget office who enters with a bachelor's degree in accounting:

	Units
Core sequence	36
Education ____ . State Education Policy Administration	4
Education ____ . Workshop in Financing Education	4
Education ____ . Introduction to Models in Social Science	4
	Total 48

A future professor of educational administration, who enters with a master's degree in administration:

	Units
Core sequence	36
Education ____ . Organizational Change and Innovation	4
Education ____ . Workshop in Financing Education	4
Education ____ . Contemporary Problems in Social Institutions	4
Education ____ . Collective Bargaining	4
Education ____ . Literature and Research in Elementary and Secondary Education	4
Education 201. History of Education in the United States	3
Education 204. Introduction to Philosophy of Education	4
Education ____ . Planning in Educational Administration	4
Education ____ . Introduction to Economics of Education	4
Education ____ . Education and Law	4
Political Science	30
Thesis	5
	Total 106

With respect to the School of Education requirements, there is no way of knowing in advance the exact number of credits that will finally be taken in each area. Stanford prides itself on the flexibility of its program, and each student largely determines his own program for the second and subsequent years, within the general confines of the above tables. Many courses apply to several area requirements at the same time. For example, the required core courses can also satisfy School of Education requirements.

Dissertation Proposals, Dissertation Committees

Students are strongly urged to begin planning for the dissertation early. There is no substitute for work that emerges out of prolonged thought about a given topic, rather than frantic, last-minute efforts to piece together a topic. Ideas for dissertations should emerge from course work, from intern experiences, from personal contact with faculty, and from research experiences. Prolonged, intense involvement is the critical factor in a successful dissertation, and the student should take the initiative for maintaining a lively dialogue about his ideas with faculty members and other students.

Once an idea has crystallized, it is time to construct a dissertation proposal. The student should consult the Guidelines for Dissertation Proposals, and also the more extensive guidelines of the Committee on Advanced Graduate Degrees. Constant dialogue with a relevant faculty member is a critical factor in preparing the proposal, for he will probably be the dissertation committee chairman and will be prepared to give advice about the proposal and the dissertation. It is up to the student to select the appropriate faculty member for his dissertation project and to secure his willingness to serve. He may or may not be the student's original adviser; the critical factor is the interest and skill of the faculty member in the student's proposed research.